MÁXIMO CASTILLO AND THE MEXICAN REVOLUTION

MÁXIMO CASTILLO

AND THE

MEXICAN
REVOLUTION

EDITED BY
JESÚS VARGAS VALDÉS

TRANSLATED BY
ANA-ISABEL ALIAGA-BUCHENAU

LOUISIANA STATE UNIVERSITY PRESS
BATON ROUGE

Published by Louisiana State University Press
Copyright © 2016 by Louisiana State University Press
All rights reserved
Manufactured in the United States of America
First printing

Designer: Barbara Neely Bourgoyne
Typeface: MillerText
Printer and binder: LSI

Map by Mary Lee Eggart.

Library of Congress Cataloging-in-Publication Data
Names: Vargas Valdez, Jesús, editor. | Aliaga-Buchenau, Ana-Isabel, translator.
Title: Máximo Castillo and the Mexican Revolution / edited by Jesús Vargas Valdés ;
    translated by Ana-Isabel Aliaga-Buchenau.
Description: Baton Rouge : Louisiana State University Press, [2016]
Identifiers: LCCN 2016012817| ISBN 978-0-8071-6388-7 (pbk. : alk. paper) | ISBN
    978-0-8071-6389-4 (pdf) | ISBN 978-0-8071-6390-0 (epub) | ISBN 978-0-8071-
    6391-7 (mobi)
Subjects: LCSH: Castillo, Máximo, 1864–1919. | Mexico—History—Revolution, 1910–
    1920—Personal narratives. | Chihuahua (Mexico : State)—History—20th century. |
    Revolutionaries—Mexico—Biography.
Classification: LCC F1234.C45155 V3713 2016 | DDC 972.08/16092—dc23
LC record available at http://lccn.loc.gov/2016012817

To don Máximo Vargas Castillo, who proudly and respectfully guarded the memoirs of his grandfather so that we could one day find out about his ideals and his actions, the true history of the causes that led to the revolution that swept up thousands of Chihuahuenses, men and women who gave their lives for a just and sovereign Mexico, respected by the other nations

CONTENTS

Illustrations follow page 72

A NOTE FROM THE TRANSLATOR

ANA-ISABEL ALIAGA-BUCHENAU

More than one hundred years after the events described in this testimonial—and six years after its first publication in Spanish—it is a great honor indeed to present an English translation of the memoirs of the Mexican revolutionary general Máximo Castillo. As the reader will learn in the successive pages, Castillo was a long-forgotten exponent of land reform in the Mexican Revolution of 1910. While other revolutionary leaders jockeyed for political position, Castillo fought primarily for the subdivision of the vast haciendas of his home state of Chihuahua. He was eventually eclipsed by more powerful revolutionary leaders, such as Francisco (Pancho) Villa and Pascual Orozco, leaders who soon thereafter found themselves on the losing end of a revolution that ended up benefitting primarily their rivals from neighboring northern states, such as Coahuila and Sonora. More than anything, this memoir reveals the complexity of the revolution in a single Mexican state.

This translation uses as its base the original Spanish-language work edited by Professor Jesús Vargas Valdés, published in Chihuahua City in 2009. As is common in Mexico, this work contains not only Castillo's original manuscript, reproduced and edited from its handwritten original, but also lengthy prefatory material. This material includes a prologue written by Professor Friedrich Katz, one of the preeminent authorities worldwide on the Mexican Revolution in general and the revolution in Chihuahua in particular, followed by three pieces authored by Professor Vargas: acknowledgments and two introductory essays. In translating these three pieces, I have kept Professor Vargas's use of the first person in order to remain as faithful as possible to the Spanish-language text. The first of the introductory essays explains how the editor found Castillo's original handwritten manuscript, and the second provides the historical background of Castillo´s life.

This translation then moves on to its primary purpose—an English-language version of Castillo's memoirs—again preserving the author's first person. I have also reproduced some of the numerous photographs in the original edition. For reasons of space, I did not translate the lengthy appendix, which includes original documents, and particularly articles from the *El Paso Morning Times* translated into Spanish from their English original.

This translated work has two sets of notes. The endnotes, designated by Arabic numerals, are translated from the original Spanish-language edition (Jesús Vargas Valdés, ed., *Máximo Castillo y la revolución en Chihuahua* [Chihuahua City: Biblioteca Chihuahuense, 2009]). The footnotes, designated by Roman numerals, are my own, and they either discuss problems of translation or supply explanations necessary for the English-language reader. While that format might prove somewhat confusing to the reader, it has the benefit of separating the translation itself—which I have striven to keep as free from comments and emendations as possible—from a small explanatory corpus that appears in the footnotes.

I appreciate the help of several individuals in bringing the project to fruition. Roger Ekirch first suggested this translation to me and brought me into contact with don Jesús Vargas, the editor of the Spanish-language edition. I appreciate Professor Vargas's permission to translate not only the memoirs but also his introductory essays, and I also thank the family of the late Friedrich Katz for permission to translate the preface that he authored. Clara Enríquez helpfully supplied many of the photographs used in this volume. This project would have been impossible without the help of Alisa Plant, Senior Acquisitions Editor; Director MaryKatherine Callaway; and Managing Editor Lee Sioles. Thanks too to Susan Murray, my fabulous copy editor. Thanks also go to Mary Eggart for creating a wonderful map. Finally, my husband, Jürgen Buchenau, brought his profound knowledge of Mexican history to bear on the project by carefully reading my translation and supplying some of the explanatory notes. I appreciate his help with some of the military and historical terminology with which he, as a specialist in the history of the Mexican Revolution, is far more familiar than I am. This translation is inspired by Nicolas Buchenau, my son, who believes in revolution.

MÁXIMO CASTILLO AND THE MEXICAN REVOLUTION

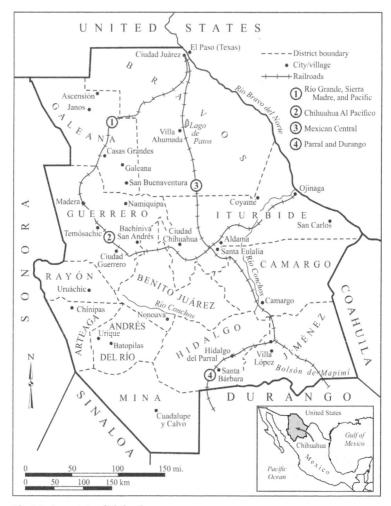

The Mexican state of Chihuahua.

PROLOGUE

FRIEDRICH KATZ

History tends to be written by the winners. To a large extent, Mexico is not an exception to this rule. The victorious Carrancista and Obregonista factions wrote most of the hefty official history of the Mexican Revolution.[i] Among the defeated, the only group that systematically attempted to justify its actions and write history from their point of view was the members of the old Porfirian oligarchy.[ii] That was not a coincidence. Many of their members were not only well educated, but they also survived their own defeat. In contrast to other revolutions, these partisans of the Old Regime generally managed to salvage not only their lives but also most of their fortunes even though they lost political power. It is perhaps ironic that while the principal leaders of the Mexican Revolution—Francisco I. Madero, Francisco Villa, Emiliano Zapata, Venustiano Carranza, and Alvaro Obregón—died violent deaths, the Porfiristas José Y. Limantour, Luis Terrazas, Enrique C. Creel, Francisco León de la Barra, Francisco Bulnes, and Jorge Vera Estañol passed away from natural causes.

To mention only two examples, not by coincidence have the works of Francisco Bulnes and Jorge Vera Estañol been so widely read and circulated. By contrast, the defeated revolutionaries who belonged to

i. These terms refer to the factions of Venustiano Carranza and General Alvaro Obregón, respectively. Both served terms as president after the victory of their factions in the revolution. The suffix –ista refers to "followers of."

ii. "Porfirian" and "Porfirista" refer to aspects and followers of the rule of the dictator Porfirio Díaz, president from 1876 to 1880 and again from 1884 to 1911. The revolution initially targeted this dictator.

1

the losing factions of the 1910–20 revolution suffered bad luck. Many of them were killed. The majority of the survivors were illiterate or semi-literate. Very few of them left memoirs, and those who did lacked the resources necessary to publish them. Zapata and his followers fared best among all the campesino revolutionaries. Even though their leader was assassinated, his followers never really met with defeat. They succeeded in seizing control of the state of Morelos, and the winners of the revolution saw themselves obligated to include them in the structure of power. That is one of the reasons—though by no means the only one—that the official history and historiography has treated Zapata much better than the northern revolutionaries who were defeated in battle.

The northern revolutionaries who opposed Carranza and Obregón were branded as bandits or simply relegated to oblivion. Although Pancho Villa could obviously not be ignored, many of the northern local leaders like Toribio Ortega and Porfirio Talamantes, from Chihuahua, or Calixto Contreras, from the Laguna region, lie forgotten in their graves. But they do not deserve such a fate. All of these men fought for many years to defend the land and rights of their villages, as witnessed in Cuchillo Parado, Janos, or San Pedro Ocuila. They were important leaders of the northern revolution and played a significant role in the defeat of the dictatorship of [General Victoriano Huerta in 1913].[iii] It is not possible to write the true history of the Mexican Revolution without understanding who these men were, why they rebelled, and the nature of their relationships with their followers as well as those whom they served.

One of the local leaders who definitely needs to be rescued from oblivion is Máximo Castillo. In contrast to almost all other revolutionary leaders in Chihuahua, he never allied himself with Villa or his División del Norte. In fact, he was an Orozquista.[iv] But also unlike most of those leaders, he never allied with the Huerta regime, either. Among the northern revolutionaries, [Castillo] was one of the greatest advocates of agrarian reform, not only in word but also in practice. He divided

---

iii. General Huerta attempted a restoration of the Porfirian dictatorship in 1913 but was defeated by a revolutionary coalition that included Carranza, Obregón, Villa, and Zapata in 1914.

iv. A follower of the fellow Chihuahuense revolutionary leader Pascual Orozco. Orozco was the head of the Chihuahuense revolutionary movement in 1910–11.

the land of six haciendas among the peasants. He was the northern revolutionary leader who felt closest to Zapata, although we do not know if he maintained any direct contact with the southerners.

[Castillo] has not been completely forgotten, but for a long time, the mention of his name conjured up descriptions of a cruel assassin, as his name was linked to one of the most horrendous crimes that occurred in Chihuahua during the revolution. In late 1913, bandits attacked a passenger train while crossing the tunnel known as "La Cumbre," with the intent of robbing it. The criminals set fire to both ends of the tunnel and impeded the exit of the passengers. Most of the passengers died from burns or asphyxiation.[v] For a long time, this crime was attributed to Máximo Castillo, even though Francisco R. Almada, the most renowned historian of Chihuahua, demonstrated long ago that Castillo had nothing to do with the crime, since he then found himself in another region of Chihuahua, far away from the scene.

The present autobiography shows a man quite different from the image of Castillo, the bandit. These memoirs describe a revolutionary who first fought for Madero[vi] and then, for Orozco. He grew disaffected with both of these caudillos. He tried to join the forces of Villa, who rejected his assistance. When he crossed the U.S. border to reorganize his forces, North American authorities arrested him. He spent a lot of time in U.S. prisons and internment camps under very difficult conditions.

These memoirs are of great interest, not only because they tell the life story of one of the most interesting revolutionaries of Chihuahua but also because of what they reveal regarding the attitudes, mentality, and history of many of the revolutionary leaders. A few of Castillo's descriptions have to be read with caution. When he wrote his memoirs, perhaps imprisoned in the United States, he was a leader who had become disillusioned with the revolution and its leaders. He was all on his own, without the help of any leader or faction. [Castillo] clearly expresses his disenchantment in his memoirs. If we allow for this fact

v. Note, however, Jesús Vargas Valdés's very different account of this accident in his introduction to this volume, "Máximo Castillo and His Times."

vi. Francisco I. Madero, the leader of the anti-Díaz coalition that began the Mexican Revolution on November 20, 1910. Madero was the revolution's first president from October 1911 to February 1913.

and remember that he was not a very well educated man whose memoirs were not written with adherence to literary norms, the account becomes a fascinating and attractive read.

Like many other Mexican revolutionaries, Castillo joined the revolution primarily because of the agrarian question. "I could not remain seated and see my comrades robbed by Porfirio Díaz's criminal agrarian laws," he declared during an interview with the *El Paso Morning Times* in February 1914. [The local authorities] "impounded their houses and threw them out into the street in the nude, just so that their tiny possessions would enlarge the great fortune of [the hacendado] Luis Terrazas." He shared some characteristics with many of the other campesino revolutionary leaders. Like Emiliano Zapata or Toribio Ortega from Cuchillo Parado, he was not a dispossessed campesino, but the owner of a small piece of land, sufficient to give him sustenance. Like Zapata and Ortega, he had traveled more than the majority of the inhabitants of his village, and he was better educated. He knew how to read and write, and he had lived in the United States for a while. His familiarity with the world beyond the confines of his native village was another aspect that he shared with other campesino revolutionaries. Ortega visited Chihuahua City and the United States; Primo Tapia, a campesino leader from Michoacán, worked as a day laborer in the United States; and Emiliano Zapata (although he never left Mexico) traveled through areas outside Morelos and visited the national capital.

Nonetheless, Castillo distinguished himself from the majority of campesino leaders: not only from those of the revolution of 1910 but also from those of the revolution of 1913–14. First, he was older than most of them, who were between twenty and thirty years old when the revolution broke out. Born in 1864, Máximo Castillo was forty-six years old when he joined Madero's revolution in 1910. Other differences loomed as even more significant. In contrast to Zapata, Heliodoro Olea Arias of Bachíniva, or Calixto Contreras from San Pedro Ocuila, Máximo Castillo insisted that the government never persecuted him for political reasons. His motive for saying so makes sense since, contrary to the experience of other leaders, Castillo never figured as the spokesperson for his village or participated in political activities. This is the most important difference between him and other Mexican campesino leaders. Zapata had been the spokesperson of Anenecuilco; Ortega, of Cuchillo Parado; Contreras, of San Pedro Ocuila . . . just to mention a few. Their involvement in their communities drove those leaders directly into conflict with the government, participation in politics, and finally, the decision to rebel. By contrast, Castillo never wanted to become the representative of his village, San Nicolás de Carretas. In fact, his memoirs describe his refusal to stand for election for the office of *presidente municipal,* or mayor, despite the encouragement of many residents. He maintained that he would not have been able to do anything for them on account of the general climate of injustice that prevailed in those days.

What, then, made him rebel? Aside from declaring, in general terms, his heartfelt opposition to the injustice and evil of Porfirian society, Castillo remains vague regarding the answer to this question. His most concrete statement concerning this matter might be the contrast that he drew between the situation of the United States and Mexico:

> Along the way, I made an observation on the coal mines and the ranches through which I passed. The poorest North Americans maintained their small houses in good order, and they had a lot of food to eat and more than enough clothes to wear. Also, along the way I saw food and clothes thrown away, and I occasionally made use of those. I asked myself: "Why is there so much misery among us Mexicans? Maybe because of our stupidity, or is our government to blame?"

Castillo was involved with three revolutionary movements in Mexico: the Maderista revolution of 1910–11; the Orozquista revolt of 1912; and the attempt to organize an independent revolutionary movement in 1913. In February 1914, without friends and isolated, he was finally imprisoned in the United States, which concluded his participation in the revolution. These experiences intensely influenced his description of revolutionary leaders, of whom none, with the exception of Emiliano Zapata, emerges with a positive image in these pages.

Nonetheless, his observations about the revolutionaries are important. Although they do not drastically change our perception of these leaders, they do give us a much more nuanced image of those men, in contrast to the postrevolutionary clichés and legends. Castillo describes Madero as extremely valiant. In the Battle of Casas Grandes, Madero refused to flee while most of his army scattered to the winds, and he would not sit or lie down while the bullets whizzed around him. When the Federal troops approached, Madero refused to mount a horse he was offered for his escape because he thought that the horse was "very skinny." Only when they offered him a horse that he found agreeable did Madero reluctantly agree to join his army in retreat. Castillo is ambivalent regarding the reasons for Madero's conduct: "I looked at the countenance of all of us. I could see the terror in the eyes of my comrades. . . . Mr. Madero's face betrayed irritation. I said to myself: 'either this gentleman does not know that bullets kill, or he is very brave.'"

Upon reading Castillo's memoirs, we can understand better why Madero trusted the Federal army that would ultimately defeat him, and specifically General Victoriano Huerta, who was responsible not only for his fall but perhaps even for his death. It shows an extremely naïve president who believed in the goodwill of his opponents. Despite pleas from his brother, Gustavo, and his mother, Madero had doubts about retaining Máximo Castillo and many other Chihuahuense revolutionaries, who had been his escort during the 1910 revolution. As he put it, "all of them loved him."

What induced Castillo to turn his back on Madero, his old boss, with whom he had been very close as his personal guard in Casas Grandes, where he even saved his life, in order to join the revolt that would later become known as the Orozquista Rebellion? In an interview with the *El Paso Morning Times*, Castillo asserted that his conduct owed to Madero's unfulfilled promises and, above all, the example of Morelos, a place he visited with a group of delegates whom Madero sent to negotiate with Zapata in 1911:

> There, I saw my dreams come true. Two vast states, Morelos and Guerrero, were building in their midst an agrarian republic after three years of continuous revolution. I saw how Zapata divided the great haciendas into small plots and gave them to men who were at once peasants and warriors, and who had rebelled to protect their land.

In his memoirs, Castillo insists that Madero's lack of gratitude toward his lower-class allies led them to rebel against his regime. He describes Madero as someone who bade good-bye to the Chihuahuense revolutionaries without a word of appreciation. The caudillo did not want to take them with him as his personal guard; rather, he had to be persuaded by his family and close collaborators. When Castillo asked for an audience with the president, Madero let him wait for weeks and, in the end, refused to see him. When he decided to return to Chihuahua, he did so as a former soldier, without any money, since the president had not even given him sufficient funds to pay for his trip. Then he joined a new rebellion in Chihuahua against Madero, directed by allies of Emilio Vázquez Gómez, which Orozco joined later on.

> I saw a copy of Orozco's Plan of Tacubaya, and it filled me with immense enthusiasm. It promised land reform . . . In the station of Gallego, I joined my forces with those of Salazar, and we met with Pascual Orozco close to Chihuahua City. There, we solemnly swore to defend the Plan of San Luis Potosí. In March, we marched toward the south as a true campesino rebellion. We took Chihuahua City.

Castillo's description of the Orozquista movement and its leaders constitutes one of the most valuable parts of his memoirs. He did not like Orozco. This antipathy and distrust in the Chihuahuense revolutionary began on the day when Orozco, who did not want to subordinate his troops to a command designated by Madero, abandoned Madero's emissaries, including his brother, Raúl, in hostile territory. His action left them in danger of being captured by government troops. At that moment, for the first time, Castillo decided to break with Orozco. Instead of retiring with Orozco's troops, he took the emissaries under his own protection and took them back to the U.S. border. Neither does Orozco look good in Castillo's depiction of his intent to arrest Madero in Ciudad Juárez in 1911. In 1912, for a short time, he appears to have believed that Orozco could be the leader who would realize the agrarian reform in Chihuahua. After all, Emiliano Zapata had recognized Orozco as the supreme leader of the new revolution. Nevertheless, Castillo soon found himself disillusioned once again when he discovered his close links with the traditional oligarchy from Chihuahua.

> Then came the most bitter moment in my life. I found out that Orozco was a traitor, a coward who had been bought by the rich. Everywhere, affluent people offered him dances and banquets. He became a hero of

high society. He accepted cash gifts from the same thieves who had left the poor without a piece of land they could call their own. One day, he told me that he did not believe at all in agrarian reform. Salazar, Rojas, and I left him immediately after a public proclamation made before the army.

In his memoirs, Castillo describes another reason why he broke with the leader of the anti-Madero revolt from Chihuahua. Even though he had a lot of money, Orozco refused to give money or food to Castillo's starving soldiers while they were fighting Federal troops together.

Castillo draws a somewhat more favorable picture of some of the lesser chiefs of the Orozquista movement; for example, Salazar. Nonetheless, he grew disenchanted with them when they decided to ally with Huerta. He felt then that they had abandoned the revolutionary cause in cynical fashion, and he decided not to recognize Huerta. This decision entailed not joining his old comrades but instead continuing the revolution on his own account. Inspired by the Zapatista example and considering himself its northern representative, Castillo began to subdivide the lands of six haciendas owned by Luis Terrazas among the sharecroppers and renters living on the land. On that occasion, he decided to ally with Villa. However, Villa not only refused his support but went as far as sending troops to combat him.

Castillo's first response to Villa's attack was a gentlemanly act. Villa's wife, Luz Corral, had gotten lost on her way to the United States and arrived at Castillo's encampment. Rather than take her hostage, he protected her and ordered his men to escort her to the United States. This gesture, however, did not stop Villa from going after Castillo to the point of routing his troops and forcing Castillo to escape by crossing the border, where he intended to reorganize his forces. There, he was captured and imprisoned by the North American authorities, which ended his revolutionary career.

Castillo's attitude toward Villa is contradictory. In general, he paints a negative picture. He describes the great wave of fear that took hold of him when he heard Villa admonish one of his subordinates for the first time "in a tone that one uses only in a barroom." This impression changed the moment that Villa greeted him and his companions with great courtesy and a "pleasant and friendly" countenance. But the negative image returned when Castillo saw Villa's men sacking the village of Santa Isabel. He confronted Villa when he, together with Orozco, attempted to arrest Madero in Ciudad Juárez, and he related how Madero ordered Villa's execution.

The impression that Castillo takes away from the confrontation between the two men is much stronger than what has generally been assumed. Thus, Madero's profound distrust of Villa becomes more understandable. Let us remember the fact that Madero refused to help Villa when he found himself prisoner in Mexico City. He felt that Villa continued to support the banditry of his followers even after the revolutionary triumph.

Despite this negative impression of Villa, Castillo intended to ally with him in 1913, but Villa rejected his request. Castillo does not explain the reasons for Villa's decision. However, by all indications, it owed at least in part to Villa's general opposition and mistrust toward anyone who had allied with Orozco. But that was not a sufficient reason: José Isabel Robles had also been an Orozquista, only to become one of Villa's most trusted generals.

One of the reasons for Villa's opposition to Castillo can be found, with difficulty, in North American sources. In contrast to Villa, Castillo did not limit his attacks to the Mexican hacendados and oligarchy in the state. Rather, he also attacked United States property. That was something that Villa had attempted to avoid at all costs since the first day he joined the revolution, because he needed arms and support from the United States. It was perhaps this issue—a political difference—that separated the two leaders more than anything else. In North American eyes, Castillo was a thief, and Villa aimed to demonstrate that he would protect U.S. property and eradicate banditry in Chihuahua.

It seems that Villa not only expelled Castillo from Chihuahua also annulled his agrarian reform. This was not due to a fundamental opposition to agrarian reform on Villa's part, but to other reasons. For one thing, Villa needed to use the revenue from the haciendas he had expropriated from Terrazas to finance his army and his revolution. For another, he felt that the sharecroppers and renters on the haciendas should not be the primary beneficiaries of agrarian reform. Instead, he favored his soldiers, who had put their lives on the line for the revolution.

When Castillo at last embarked on his trip to the United States in early 1914, practically alone and without friends, he left the revolution as he had entered it: poor and without money. The only contrarian perspective to the image of a bandit that has so often been applied to him comes from eminent historians such as Francisco R. Almada, who clarify that Castillo did not have any involvement in the bloody incident of La Cumbre. They also point out the fact that—in contrast to many other revolutionary leaders—Castillo never used the power and the resources at his disposal to enrich himself during the age of revolution. His memory truly needs to be rescued from oblivion, and these memoirs will contribute to that endeavor to a significant extent. They are a living testimonial of the history of the great popular revolution that swept Mexico, and particularly Chihuahua, beginning in 1910.

INTRODUCTORY MATERIAL

JESÚS VARGAS VALDÉS

ACKNOWLEDGMENTS

In its process of creation, every book of historical research is the product of collective contribution. Despite appearances, and regardless of what some may say to the contrary, the strictly individual work does not exist. In the end, the worth of an author's work consists in searching, integrating, systematizing, and editing the information, the data dispersed in documents and testimonials. Once this process has concluded, the work continues: revisions, corrections, printing, distribution, etc.

Ten years ago, we began the work that led to the publication of the memoirs of General Máximo Castillo. For that reason, we run the risk of omitting in the acknowledgments the names of some of the people who helped directly with the process. If such omissions have occurred, we apologize in advance, recognizing that this book would never have been published without the effort and enthusiasm of many people who helped us.

In the first place, we recognize and thank Sr. Máximo Vargas Castillo for his participation, and especially for his trust in allowing us access to the original document, as well as for his generosity in sharing the photos of his family archive with us. We also thank his late sister, Nati, who originally told us about the existence of her grandfather's memoirs.

[We also appreciate the help of] Diana Bueno Hernández, who took charge of organizing each sheet of the original document chronologically. She also made the first copy of the document as well as the first revision, the organization of the appendices, the timeline, and the preparation of the biographical and geographical references.

[We thank] Doctor Friedrich Katz for the prologue and for his generosity in sharing with us a large number of documents that he found in archives of the United States; as well as Juan Agustín Romero, who translated documents and newspaper articles related to the activities of General Máximo Castillo in the Mexican Revolution in Chihuahua from English to Spanish.

From the beginning and all the way to the end of this investigation, we relied on the disinterested help of many people whose valuable cooperation we recognize and appreciate: Abelardo Amaya, Rosa María Arroyo, José Guadalupe Cadena, José Guadalupe Celís, Guadalupe Chacón, Fernando del Moral, Willivaldo Delgadillo, Alfredo Espinosa, Margarita Flores, the late Daniel Fourzán, William French, Apolinar Frías, Flor García, Carlos González H., Eva Lucrecia Herrera, the late Humberto Icaza, Jane Dale Lloyd, Manuel López Chacón, Karla Martínez, Alma Montemayor, Margarita Muñoz, Regina Navarro, Ramón Navarro Salazar, Víctor Orozco, Rubén Osorio, Jesús Antonio Pinedo, the late Segundo Portilla, Martha Ramos, Víctor Hugo Rascón, Rubén Armando Rico, Luis Carlos Salcido, María Isabel Sen Venero, Micaela Solís, Ricardo Torres, and Mónica Villegas. Special and constant appreciation and recognition go to Marcela Frías Neve.

Our thanks go also to those who participated in the organization of the presentation of this book, which took place on February 12, 2004, with the assistance of Alma Montemayor and María Isabel Sen Venero as commentators, and Lic. Guadalupe Chacón Monárrez as the coordinator of the event.

INTRODUCTION

[As of this writing,] the revolution of 1910 began almost one hundred years ago. In the minds of many Mexicans, this chapter of national history remains relevant. Several of the principal protagonists and events involved in ten long years of civil war that embroiled all Mexicans in direct or indirect fashion continue to elicit emotion and interest. With new perspectives, historians sift through an array of documentary sources, and much of what was long regarded as unquestionable truth has since been called into question, reconsidered, and even subjected to documentary verification. In the last few years, the interest has increased, especially in those areas where the revolution encountered its greatest social response and where the devastation of war left the deepest wounds. That is the case with Chihuahua. Recently, [historians] have pursued lines of investigation that had previously received no attention; for example, case studies of villages that produced the first contingents who rebelled because of the alienation of *ejido*, or village property. They also focused on other previously unstudied factors that contributed to the social unrest. Among those factors, one could mention the prerevolutionary electoral process or the mobilization of several villages against the high taxes imposed by Porfirian authorities. Recent research has also underscored the importance of testimonial documents. Some of these testimonials were published in magazines, newspapers, and even in self-published editions: some had very small print runs; others have been forgotten. As a result of this new interest, a large number of new works has enriched the bibliographies of regional [history]. The state of Chihuahua has witnessed a notable increase in publications that present new essays, biographies, accounts, and stories, as well new editions of books printed in small editions many years ago.[1] With respect to the testimonials printed in modest self-published editions, we find works such as those by Heliodoro Olea, Teodosio Duarte, and Francisco Ontiveros. But there are also other works never before published, as is the case with the present work entitled *Máximo Castillo and the Mexican Revolution*.[2]

The case of Máximo Castillo was that of thousands of Chihuahuenses who went to fight for the ideal of change. These people thought that the government of Porfirio Díaz was the primary culprit responsible for Mexico's backwardness as well as for injustice and the absence of democracy. At the age of forty-six, [Castillo] was one of the first to take up arms in 1910. But before continuing with the history of the person, it is important to write a few lines about the testimonial and the circumstances that led us to this document.

The Encounter with Máximo Castillo's Memoirs

In the exercise of searching and finding, the historian simultaneously constructs his own historical timeline by recording memorable moments, successes and failures, curiosities and anecdotes, disappointments and rewards. The job of a historian resembles that of a prospector, who submerges himself in subterranean tunnels with nothing more than a small flame lighting his way, convinced that sooner or later he will find what he seeks: the gold thread, the shimmer that indicates the presence of the coveted metal. What drives the prospector is not the value of the gold, but the encounter. Similarly, the historian searches for the purpose of finding. Between the "lost" documents and the researcher, there is a force field of "magnetic attraction" that almost always leads to the encounter. In general, it is the investigator who reaches his objective, the document; but in a few cases, it is the document that finds the investigator. To a certain extent, that is what happened to us with the memoirs of General Máximo Castillo.

In 1987, while we were working to gather bibliographical information to write the book *Historia mínima de Chihuahua*, we first encountered Máximo Castillo's name in Benjamín Herrera Vargas's book *La revolución en Chihuahua, 1910–1911*. This work presents a few general facts with regard to the agrarian redistribution undertaken by General Castillo in 1913, two months earlier than General Lucio Blanco's historic agrarian reform [reputed to be the very first in the nation]. This piece of information impressed us, and from then on, we set about looking for more evidence. A few days later, we found more information about General Castillo's biography in the books of [the historian] Francisco Almada.

Later on, in 1988, we interviewed Mr. Sabino Torres at his home, who distinguished himself as one of the initiators of railroad unionism in Chihuahua. On that occasion, we made the acquaintance of his wife, Mrs. Nati Vargas, who told us that she was the granddaughter of General Máximo Castillo and that her grandfather had left a few handwritten accounts. Doña Nati showed us a photograph in which [Castillo] appeared at the side of President Francisco I. Madero. We had seen other photos of Castillo, but that particular one impressed us because the face reflected nobility, loyalty, and triumphant pride . . . In the gaze of the general, we found condensed, symbolically, the state of mind of a people at arms who, tired of injustice, concentrated all of its hopes and desires in a leader it committed to follow until death: Francisco I. Madero.

After this conversation, doña Nati, the granddaughter of the general, promised us that she would talk to her brother, Máximo Vargas Castillo, and urge him to allow us to take a glimpse at "the papers." Nonetheless, time passed without the opportunity to see those memoirs. On that occasion, there was no continuity or follow-up, because at that time, we had committed our mind and pen to a study of the history of syndicalism in the state of Chihuahua. Our attention was entirely focused on that endeavor, and we forgot about doña Nati's offer.

A year passed until we encountered Máximo Castillo's name once again in the second half of 1988. While we were researching the journalistic archive of *El Heraldo* (period 1928–40), we found a note from March 8, 1938, regarding a tribute to don Abraham González. The official speaker of the event, don Daniel Fourzán, remembered that the meetings to prepare the uprising of November 20, 1910, were held in Máximo Castillo's house. He said the following:

> In the now populous neighborhood of Santo Niño, on 3108 José Eligio Muñoz, there is—just as it was thirty years ago—the humble abode of Máximo Castillo, looking just as abandoned as ever. This little house was the nest from where many of the great revolutionary eagles rose up, powerful and bent on conquest.

As soon as we read the note, we left the newspaper building and immediately went to look for the address. Almost eighty years later, the Santo Niño neighborhood had changed a great deal. Nonetheless, we imagined an adobe hut, and with pure intuition, we went to José Eligio Muñoz Street. Indeed, at number 3108, we found a modest adobe hut in ruins, the door unhinged and buried under half a meter of trash, and the lot covered with weeds. Without much thought, we knocked on the door of the house next door. An amiable lady opened the door, and we asked her if she knew who owned the neighboring walls. She told us it belonged to her husband, Mr. Máximo Vargas. We asked her to let him know that we were interested in talking to him.

That was how we finally made contact with the brother whom doña Nati had mentioned, the grandson of General Castillo and the keeper of his grandfather's "papers." Once we had introduced ourselves and explained the reason for our visit, he pleasantly answered each of our questions while we explained to him what we knew about his grandfather. Then he showed us an envelope containing photographs and the original document, written in 1915 in the prison of Fort Wingate in the United States. We talked the entire afternoon and finally dared to ask him if we would be able to make a copy of the text someday. With an amiable and frank smile, Sr. Máximo Vargas told us that we could use the document right away with the warning to take very good care of it. Thus began a friendship that allowed us to get better acquainted with the personality of General Castillo by means of his descendants as well as the memories and assorted anecdotes transmitted from generation to generation.

With this knowledge, we searched for [Castillo's] name in the encyclopedias of the Mexican Revolution as well as in books about the history of the region, and we only found general information about his life. We finally concluded that existing writings about his participation left the impression of a controversial figure. Some authors treated him like a hero, while others described him as a mean-spirited murderer. For example, in the biographical dictionary of the well-known historian Francisco R. Almada, he appears as a hero who saved Francisco I. Madero's life during the Battle of Casas Grandes.[3] On the other hand, the book *Chihuahua: Almacén de tempestades* refers to him as a murderer. The authors of that work, Florence and Robert Lister, have this to say about Castillo:

> An extortionist, self-aggrandizing gunman, Castillo reigned ruthlessly by means of terrorism . . . His band lay in ambush until a train of more than fifty passengers entered the Cumbre Tunnel, south of Pearson, and detonated dynamite charges at both ends. All the people on the train died from burns or asphyxiation by the clouds of smoke that saturated the tunnel. Many of the victims were North Americans who worked in the forestry enterprises in the sierra.[4]

Francisco Ontiveros, the author of the testimonial book *Toribio Ortega y la Brigada González Ortega*, is even more critical than the Listers. From the pages of this book, we will extract three particularly judgmental paragraphs that refer to Castillo. Through this judgment, one can see the extent to which disagreements and rancor made mortal enemies out of people who came from the same social class and from among the same people. In 1914, when Castillo was still a prisoner in Fort Wingate, New Mexico, in the United States, Ontiveros wrote:

Máximo Castillo is a bandit who has never had a banner or fought for any ideal. He devotes himself to the pillage and rape of defenseless villages, acting under the name of the ridiculous, cowardly Vázquez Gómez. He remained under Salazar's command during the coup d'état in Mexico City. Once Salazar recognized [the Huerta regime, Castillo] left him, foreseeing that he would no longer be able to exercise his profession of thief in the small towns and villages. Accompanied by Braulio Hernández, a rascal of the first order who hailed from one of those miserable corners of the great cities, he went on the road to wait for defenseless pedestrians and ask them for their purse or their life.

Pompously, Castillo had his followers call him "General in Chief of the Northern Revolution," and with this title, he asked General Villa to join him. Villa replied by asking him for a meeting, but the Generalísimo was no longer joking. When he parted ways with Salazar, he had four hundred men with him, but all of them deserted because of the role they played alongside a crazy, nutty old man who was the puppet of an ambitious cheater. When he arrived at Casas Grandes, he had no more than one hundred men.

General Villa resolved to put an end to the Harlequinesque general once and for all, and sent Majors Santiago Ramírez and Porfirio Talamantes to defeat him. The two officers attacked him and roundly defeated him. They took prisoners, pardoning all of them except one who called himself colonel, who was shot during the action.[5]

In [Benjamín Herrera's] book, titled *Aquí Chihuahua! Cuna y chispa de la revolución mexicana*, a caption underneath a photograph of Castillo states the following:

. . . He was chief of the honor escort of don Francisco I. Madero in April and May 1911. In 1912, he became an Orozquista partisan. He began his first land reform on June 5, 1913. On June 11, 1913, he attacked the Pearson train station, violating the hospitality that the United States had offered him. On February 4, 1914, he attacked and robbed a train of the Noroeste de México, setting fire to and dynamiting the Cumbre Tunnel. Fifty-one passengers died.[6]

The above references are all that the regional historiography has recuperated: a series of contradictory judgments about a figure who remained almost unknown even though in many photographs, his singular face and stature appear at the side of Francisco I. Madero as well as other Chihuahuense revolutionaries.

Months later, when we had already acquired much more information, we suggested to don Máximo Vargas a meeting with his sons and grandsons so that we could tell them—and especially the young adults and children of his family—about this man who had died for his ideals. Vargas accepted with great enthusiasm. The meeting was on a Sunday afternoon. All of the sons and daughters of don Máximo Vargas were in attendance with their respective families. Although all of the adults knew the story of the grandfather, the retelling of this story by an outsider, an investigator who attempted to explain every one of Castillo's steps and political decisions, was something that enriched family history. It particularly enthralled the youngsters, who knew only the basic facts.

Considering the autobiographical information that the general left in his memoirs as well as what we had been able to find out about him until then, we had enough information to explain the career of the general, which we can sum up in the following manner. Until just before 1910, Sr. Máximo Castillo led a life of hard work dedicated to his wife and children. In 1910, he converted his blacksmithing shop into a meeting center for a group of anti-reelectionists.[i] Most of them were neighbors from Santo Niño. The principal organizer of these meetings was a railroad worker, Cástulo Herrera, and according to Daniel Fourzán's memoirs, Mr. Abraham González attended these meetings a few times. Since the first moments of the armed rebellion against the Porfirian dictatorship, Máximo Castillo completely dedicated himself to the tasks that he faced as organizer, combatant, and later on, as a smuggler responsible for moving a load of arms and ammunition from the U.S. border, which he personally handed over to Pascual Orozco.

i. The "anti-reelectionists" was the name given to Madero's movement. Madero's rallying cry was "effective suffrage, no reelection," in reference to Porfirio Díaz's multiple terms in the presidential chair.

During the first months of 1911, he was the chief of the personal escort of Francisco I. Madero. In February 1912, he signed the Plan of Santa Rosa, and the following month, he signed the Plan of the Empacadora, both in Chihuahua City. In 1913, he headed the Zapatista movement in the state of Chihuahua, and at the beginning of 1914, he was identified as the responsible party in a criminal act that claimed dozens of lives.

General Castillo Speaks Out

While Máximo Castillo was imprisoned in Fort Bliss and Fort Wingate, he sat down to write what he had experienced during four years of revolutionary activity. We know little about what happened afterward. His family did not want to preserve sad memories; all that remained was the old manuscript, handwritten in pencil, and a few blots that indicated the lack of an eraser.

Eighty-eight years after their creation, these memoirs are now finally seeing the light of day, thus fulfilling the wishes of General Máximo Castillo. The memoirs contribute the perspective of a protagonist to the regional and national historiography, a protagonist who may be considered a representative of all those campesinos, cowboys, and workers who coalesced in the revolutionary armies with no other desire than to transform Porfirian Mexico. These memoirs constitute an excellent historical document, not only because of their testimonial character but also because the author leads the reader through the principal moments and movements that characterized the revolution in the state of Chihuahua.

Here we see a real revolutionary, a human being who makes the decision to enter the revolution because he had made an honorable promise the prior year, and because it seemed to him that things needed to change even though he did not know how. Before joining the revolution, he had to confront his family, which opposes his intention and reproaches him for abandoning his wife and children. In addition, the author, as a member of the inner circle, introduces us to a very different Francisco I. Madero than the one whom historians have known until today. In his position as chief of escort, Castillo established a close relationship with the leader, his family, and his principal collaborators. Although Castillo remained absolutely loyal, he was aware that accompanying the leader would allow him to be very close to the new government in order "to see that the goals for which [Mexicans] had made the revolution would be accomplished." But that did not happen. After he arrived in Mexico City, Madero forgot his escort, who had to return to Chihuahua disillusioned and now convinced that the revolution had gotten off track.

Máximo Castillo's version of Francisco I. Madero is a real-life personality shorn of the vestments and halo of the "political saint" created by the official historiography. He is a revolutionary leader who initially awakened civic consciousness and attracted the support of thousands of Mexicans; a leader ready to die for his ideals but also a man whose political and ideological formation took place in very different circumstances than those prevailing in rural Mexico at the time. With a little bit of naiveté, but naturally and convincingly, Castillo paints a portrait of a leader who did not correctly interpret the desires of a people that had placed all of its trust in him. A reading of these memoirs reveals how Madero, little by little, cast off the revolutionary leaders who had brought him to power, while opportunistic politicians and Porfirian military leaders took over the leadership of the new revolutionary government. After many attempts to remain at Madero's side, Castillo, disappointed and convinced that the revolution had lost its way, signed the Plan of Santa Rosa in February 1912 together with Professor Braulio Hernández. A short while later, he signed the Plan of the Empacadora headed by General Pascual Orozco.

This change of mind was not the product of a sudden emotional insight but, rather, the reaction of the majority of the Chihuahuenses. In the same vein, the Chihuahuenses interpreted Madero's choice of José María Pino Suárez as his vice-presidential candidate over Dr. Francisco Vázquez Gómez as an imposition. When Castillo wrote the corresponding part of his memoirs, he clearly justified the reasons for and motives driving the new revolutionary movement.

That year, Castillo got to know several of the leaders known as Orozquistas. In a simple manner, his memoirs describe his opinions of several of these leaders, such as J. Inés Salazar, Campa, and Orozco himself. Among all the chiefs whom he met during that time, he recognized the greatest revolutionary merits in two of them: Abelardo Amaya and César Canales. Both died the same day during a combat in Durango, and in Castillo's opinion, the revolution lost two of its greatest leaders at that moment. The original document consists of forty-two notebook pages written in a very small, narrow hand. The manuscript is hard to read because it was written in pencil, and the writing has faded over time. Most of the pages were out of order, and it is almost certain that the last one or two pages were lost. In order to present these memoirs to the public, Diana Bueno dedicated herself to the task of putting the pages in chronological order. She then deciphered and transcribed them line by line, processes that required several weeks of intense work. For reasons beyond our control, publication was delayed even though we completed the work on the original manuscript in 1990. But the delay allowed us to enrich the information and enlarge the documentary sources.

The reader will be able to see that Máximo Castillo set about writing his memoirs with the intention of leaving his perspective to posterity: because he was a man of honor; because they had unjustly accused him; because he did not want his name to remain compromised; because he did not want to leave a stain on his family. Patiently and in very small letters, he wrote down the most important parts of his biography as well as the revolutionary cause that he had supported. Above all, he was concerned with the destiny of the revolution and the good memory of his name. In these memoirs, we find a Chihuahuense who was with the Zapatistas and then wanted to apply in Chihuahua the land redistributions of Morelos. We see a disillusioned man who felt betrayed by Madero and who joined the Orozco Rebellion of 1912. The following year, he refused to recognize the Victoriano Huerta regime and concluded that Orozco, too, had betrayed the revolution.

It was most likely in December 1915, after the U.S. authorities had notified him that he would be set free, that he gave the manuscript to his wife, María de Jesús, thinking that the memoirs would be published someday and his honor and integrity would be saved. After the death of doña María de Jesús, the pages passed on to his daughter, who in turn gave the document and various photographs to Máximo Vargas, the grandson of the general. For years, the fragile pages of the memoirs survived the neglect and the passage through many curious and naïve hands that did not properly appreciate the significance of those lines written in "old handwriting." Don Máximo, the last custodian of the papers, kept them together with the photographs. It was he who finally fulfilled the wishes of his grandfather in the sense that his words would be heard.

Ninety-two years after the signing of the Constitution of 1917, and ninety-one years after these memoirs were written, the name of Máximo Castillo emerges. Castillo speaks out to tell us about another revolution, one that he lived and that featured protagonists from among the people, real men who rose up like the dust devils of the northern plains, erasing everything in their path. General Castillo speaks out on behalf of thousands of revolutionaries who disappeared silently. He speaks out to talk about himself, to tell the story of an idealistic man who became the shadow of Francisco I. Madero, as the chief escort after the defeat in Casas Grandes on March 6, 1911.

He wrote in his memoirs that at one time, when his wife was visiting him in Fort Wingate, he let her know what he thought of himself. Among other things, he told her: "If they kill me, my body will die, but my memory will persist alive for all times, like that of Hidalgo, like that of Juárez, or like that of a bandit . . ." Did Castillo lose his bet? Did his name remain as that of a bandit? Has history forgotten his presence? By reading the pages that follow, where he tells of his experiences in the revolution as well as his role in the historical events and his relationship with some of the principal figures, the reader will find the necessary elements to make up his or her own mind.

After much thought, we decided to add additional data under the title of "Introductory Study" [titled "Máximo Castillo and His Times" in the present volume] with the intention of giving the reader complementary information for better comprehension of this very important document. But we do not consider that section indispensable reading. If the reader desires to proceed immediately to the document of General Castillo, the value of the same will not find itself reduced in any way.

Finally, we consider it advisable to inform the readers that the notes as well as the sections and documents appended to the memoirs were written more than ten years ago. We decided not to modify anything with respect to the original purpose of this work, conserving the emotional charge and spontaneity of those years in the early 1990s when we began to investigate the field of the regional history of Chihuahua.

MÁXIMO CASTILLO AND HIS TIMES [ii]
Sowers of the Wind

At the turn of the new century, the capitalists of Chihuahua joyfully celebrated the economic success of their enterprises and business. From the watchtower from which they observed the general situation in Mexico, and particularly Chihuahua, everything was fine. Food production was sufficient to feed the people, and there was lots of work on the great haciendas and mines as well as in the factories of the city. If someone was not working, it was because he or she did not feel like making an effort at all. And if someone committed a crime, however minor, they received rigorous punishment, because the authorities believed that everything depended on the maintenance of public order.

Nonetheless, since the late nineteenth century, the jails were packed full of poor people who had either become thieves or rebelled in different ways against the Porfirian system. Day after day, new groups of rustlers and muggers emerged or joined the existing gangs. Thus, in a parallel development to the progress of capitalism, there emerged a countervailing movement in the entire state, and the owners of capital did not notice it.

Carried forth by ambition, a few great hacendados took advantage of the new laws concerning fallow land. With the help of the land surveying companies, they expropriated hundreds of rancheros who had never received a title to their land from either the colonial Spanish or the national Mexican government. That is how many rancheros who had lived and worked on their land for generations found themselves helpless when the attorneys of the surveying companies demanded that they present their property titles. In the Porfirian legal system,

ii. The original title of this section is "Estudio Introductorio," or introductory study. Upon the recommendation of the editorial staff at the Louisiana State University Press, I have provided a more explanatory title, which also clarifies Professor Vargas's choice to provide two separate introductions.

they had no legal defense against these abuses. [The landowners] also seized many of the old village *ejidos*, and thus, many young men who had never been hacienda peons, but were rancheros who worked their own land and tended to their own herds, lost their means of subsistence overnight. They deeply resented the government of Porfirio Díaz, which they held primarily responsible for all of the unjust actions.

In the large cities, discontent also grew, because every four years, it was the same old story: General Díaz was reelected for another term, and blood and fire drenched any demonstration of dissent or in favor of democracy. But the capitalists did not notice that, either. For them, everything was fine. It was natural that the people resented order and progress and protested against it. The law and the army existed for that very purpose. These conditions of social unrest and blindness on the part of the capitalists in power spawned the first prerevolutionary movements: for example, the one in Tomóchic (1891–92), or the ones in Temósachic and Santo Tomás, in 1893. In many other locations in the state, popular rebellions broke out more or less spontaneously and more or less violently.

One of the characteristics of these prerevolutionary movements was that they specifically demanded the return to the constitutional order of 1857. From that perspective, they called upon the people to topple the primary obstacle thereto: the Porfirian dictatorial government. At the same time as in Chihuahua, other states also featured various insurgent movements during the last decade of the century, but all of them remained spontaneous and isolated.

In this context, Mexican liberals convoked the Congress of San Luis Potosí with the objective of founding a new party called Partido Liberal Mexicano.[7] Among those at the forefront of the organizing council, three brothers—Ricardo, Enrique, and Jesús Flores Magón—distinguished themselves. For Chihuahua, two delegates attended who were members of the Club Liberal of Hidalgo del Parral. Later on, a large number of like-minded people from all over the state joined this nucleus, for example, Elfego, José, and Jesús Lugo, young inhabitants of the town of Parral who took on a primary role in the fight against the Porfirian dictatorship.

Members of the Partido Liberal earned the monikers "Magonistas" or "anarchists." The latter term made reference to the increasingly aggressive character of their revolutionary objectives. Although the original aims of the Partido Liberal Mexicano had been legalist-democratic in nature, circumstances had pushed its partisans toward more and more radical positions within a few years.

The principal weapon of the Partido Liberal was the newspaper *Regeneración*, the official publication of the organization, which publicized not only the ideas of party members but also those of many readers who expressed complaints and concerns about the dictatorship. Beginning in 1904, the distribution of this newspaper in the state of Chihuahua increased noticeably alongside the number of rancheros and workers ready to take up arms against the authorities and the soldiers of the Porfirian army.

Before the emergence of the anti-reelectionist struggle convoked by Francisco I. Madero, it was the organizers of the Partido Liberal Mexicano who pushed the Mexican people to fight against the dictatorship with heroism and bravery. Although only few historians have been interested in studying the antecedents of the revolution of 1910, it can be said that the Magonistas of the Partido Liberal were the primary agents who prepared the way for Francisco I. Madero to come to power.[iii] During the years before the revolution, members of this party established a political relationship with Francisco I. Madero. Nonetheless, after 1906, they completely abandoned this alliance because they did not believe that elections were the way to defeat the dictatorship. At that moment, the Magonistas had arrived at the conclusion that it was necessary to immediately organize an armed struggle in all of the country, and they said so in the pages of the newspaper *Regeneración*.

Thus, in that same year of 1906, the leadership of the Partido Liberal organized the first attempt at general insurrection in Ciudad Juárez. Unfortunately, [the authorities] arrested the principal ringleaders and tried

---

iii. This historiographical statement was not correct even at the time of its writing. See, for example, James C. Cockcroft, *Precursors of the Mexican Revolution, 1900–1913* (Austin: University of Texas Press, 1968), which specifically studies the Magonistas as a precursor movement of the revolution. Cockcroft's book appeared in Spanish in 1971.

and convicted them in that city. The search warrants issued by the police included lists of other Chihuahuense partisans, and the resulting intense persecution led to the incarceration of dozens of sympathizers. Some of them were taken to San Juan Ulúa, as was the case with Heliodoro Olea, who would later join the anti-reelectionist cause.[8]

Two years after this fiasco, in 1908, the [PLM] organized a new, simultaneous uprising in various cities of the nation. In the case of Chihuahua, they concentrated their activities in the district of Galeana. The leader of the uprising was Práxedis Guerrero, who spearheaded a movement in the Casas Grandes region that included dozens of revolutionaries. This new attempt featured the PLM leadership of the different districts of the state, as well as Práxedis Guerrero, Santana Pérez, José Inés Salazar, and Manuel Orozco. In early May 1908, a report from the *jefe político*[iv] to the state governor related a seditious movement in the district of Galeana and presumed the involvement of members of the police force except for its chief.

The police and state government were fully aware of the insurrectionary movement of 1908. June 30 was slated as the start date, and, in the case of Chihuahua, military action took place in the Palomas customshouse. Coahuila saw fighting in Viezca and Las Vacas. In all three cases, government forces easily defeated the rebels.

Almost all of the revolutionaries who attacked Palomas came from the district of Galeana. According to the reports and communications of the authorities, fifty armed men crossed over from the United States border on June 30 after camping out for forty-eight hours in territory belonging to the State of Texas. The police chief of Palomas reported: "The bandits brought two cases of 30–30 carbines (50 rifles)." This strategy did not yield good results, as government troops entrenched themselves on the roof of the customshouse and forced the rebels to retreat. In this encounter, the rebels suffered the loss of Otilio Madrid as a result of an act of exaltation and sacrifice. At a critical moment, this young man, a comrade of Práxedis Guerrero, emerged in plain view. As a result, he was shot in the chest. When the rebels retreated, Madrid was still alive.

---

iv. Mexican term for political bosses; more specifically, a regional boss with state and national patronage.

He was interrogated and probably tortured. It remains unknown whether he died as a result of this injury or whether they killed him after the interrogation. On July 13, 1908, the state governor announced that thirty-four convicts from Galeana had arrived at the penitentiary. They stayed there until January 15, 1909, when they were "embarked" on a train to Mexico City, and from there, to the port of Veracruz.

According to the sources we have consulted, none of the thirty-four political prisoners sent to Veracruz took part in the attack on the Palomas customshouse. By all indications, the group under the leadership of Práxedis Guerrero went to the sierra of Corral de Piedras, and the majority of them crossed the border. From the United States, they continued to carry out proselytizing and organizing activities in the districts Galeana, Bravos, and Guerrero.

Although they had not reached their objectives, these experiences proved formative in the emergence of the first revolutionary armies that would join the anti-reelectionist cause two years later. Beginning in 1909, the electoral anti-reelectionist movement led by Francisco I. Madero developed rapidly at the national level. The state of Chihuahua witnessed the formation of clubs, not only in the major cities but also in a few towns of the sierra and plains.

In Parral, Guerrero, Chihuahua, and Ciudad Juárez, anti-reelectionism found widespread expression, so much so that the Porfirian authorities of that state came to consider the possibility of a Madero victory in several districts. In the days before the July 1910 elections, various *jefes políticos* and the interim governor of the state of Chihuahua, José María Sánchez, wrote to Enrique Creel in Mexico City, informing him that the *jefe político* of the Hidalgo district, Rodolfo Valles, was afraid of the results of the elections in Parral due to the level of Maderista activities. Sánchez shared this concern, but he was also worried about Guerrero, where he had sent fifty men as reinforcements under the orders of General Plata, bringing the number of military personnel in that location up to a total of ninety.

In Guerrero, Creel's principal ally was don Joaquín Chávez, who had distinguished himself in the course of more than twenty years through his efficacy in the forcible suppression of dissent among the people of the sierra. With a letter dated June 11, 1910, Enrique Creel asked Governor Sánchez to assign fifty men to Captain Joaquín Chávez, who should occupy them as if they were his workers "in order not to cause alarm." At the end of this letter, Creel appraised the situation thusly: "Well, the Guerrero district is where there might be some risk, because, as you know, there are many men under arms with resolve once they commit to a political movement."[9]

The elections took place on July 10, 1910. Despite the popular mobilization, Porfirio Díaz was declared the nationwide winner with 18,625 votes, against 186 for Madero.[10] These results constituted a new act of mockery and demonstrated that the Magonistas had been right when they said that voting would not change anything. In the following days, the discontent among the Chihuahuenses increased due to the use of repressive measures against teachers and public servants from the municipalities who had taken an open stance against the reelection of Díaz and for Madero's candidacy.

Creel acted in Mexico City as secretary of foreign relations, but with regard to the political authorities of Chihuahua, he served as an intermediary between them and the secretary of war. This becomes obvious by reading a few letters that Secretary Creel sent from Mexico City to different leaders in the state, recommending, among other things, the firing of the teachers who had actively participated as anti-reelectionists. A letter to Governor José María Sánchez dated July 1, 1910, for example, recommended the dismissal of the principal of the Escuela Oficial de Aldama, J. B. Quezada, "for having made propaganda against the government."[11] A letter dated July 4, also to Governor Sánchez, suggested the firing of Emeterio Esquivel, assistant principal of the Escuela Oficial 99, "for having behaved in a disloyal manner during the elections."[12] In a letter dated July 5, Creel indicated that the behavior of the authorities of Santa Isabel should not be ignored, and yet another letter from July 9 addressed the subject of the mayor of Moris, Isidoro Caraveo, whom he accused of participation on the anti-reelectionist side. As Creel pointed out, "one should not lose this good opportunity to eliminate all those elements who constitute a danger in the posts that they have been conferred . . . [T]he government needs to use all of its constitutional faculties to replace the bad elements with people of trust."[13]

In these conditions, one could hear ever-louder calls in favor of armed struggle. The Plan of San Luis Potosí was released in October,[v] and various groups formed in response to this revolutionary proclamation, especially in those towns where the anti-reelectionist movement had found its greatest expression. As an example of this, we can mention the fact that on October 31, Orozco visited the hardware store of Krakauer, Zork, and Moye, in Chihuahua City, in order to buy a first-rate rifle. To that end, one of the employees, Jesús Elías—a friend of Orozco's—asked him in a low voice if he was already going to fight for Madero. The future hero responded: "I will not fight for Madero, but for the rights of the people."[14]

Scenes of War

In Chihuahua, the Maderista revolutionary movement found a more or less generalized response. In some districts, the political and social conditions made this response more intense and ongoing. For example, Guerrero and Galeana featured various prerevolutionary uprisings dating from the 1890s such as those in Tomóchic and Temósachic in the former case, and in Namiquipa and Ascensión in the latter.

Among the revolutionary leaders who emerged in this first phase, one can also make a generalization: in the majority of cases, they were small rural property owners. Typical cases included Abraham González, Braulio Hernández, Cástulo Herrera, Guillermo Baca, Juan Baca, Pedro T. Gómez, Fortunato Casavantes, Juan Dozal, Elfego Bencomo, Francisco Salido, Baudillo Caraveo and his brother, José María, J. Dolores Palomino, José de la Luz Blanco, Sóstenes Beltrán, Félix Terrazas, Marcelo Caraveo, Heliodoro Olea, Máximo Castillo, Luis A. García, Albino Frías, and Pascual Orozco Vázquez, among others. Most of them were men of ideas and, generally speaking, read and wrote well. A few of them, including Dozal and Casavantes, had attended school in the United States. In terms of religion, it is also important to mention that a few of them belonged to Protestant congregations, including Marcelo Caraveo, José de la Luz Blanco, Albino Frías, and Pascual Orozco.

v. Francisco I. Madero's plan for a national insurrection, which touched off the revolution on November 20, 1910.

All of these midlevel leaders were people who, like Máximo Castillo, aspired for a progressive Mexico that could compete with the neighbors to the north. Their observations and recognition of the conditions of underdevelopment in Mexico compared to [the United States] influenced their convictions to a significant degree. They desired a more productive, democratic society, without corruption and hoarding. That is to say, a society quite different from the one created in the crucible of the Porfiriato.

Roque Estrada, the secretary of Francisco I. Madero, left to posterity a very interesting observation about the prevailing conditions in the state of Chihuahua in 1910, particularly with regard to the social class that predominated among the anti-reelectionists. He recognized that oppression was less intense than in other states:

> I have more confidence in these people, moderate, serene, and respectful, than in those enthusiasts and hotheads. In addition, the Partido Antirreleccionista here mainly consists of the middle class, and that makes me suppose that it will become formidable and decisive. Whenever the insurrection breaks out, I think that our most legitimate hope lives in in Chihuahua. In addition to the reasons I have indicated, its communion with the United States facilitates the insurrectionary movement. Because anti-reelectionism [in Chihuahua] mainly consists of the middle class, its conviction will impel it to solve the problem with those means that the government will place at its disposal. Those means cannot be any other than those suggested by force, and the lesser degree of oppression that one observes will facilitate the preparation of the uprising.[15]

This opinion is key to a characterization of the leadership of the revolution in the state of Chihuahua. Hundreds of hacienda peons made up the social revolutionary base along with inhabitants of small ranches that had drifted downward due to the surveying companies and a few mine and railroad workers. In general, however, [the movement] consisted of elements that had a place in the regional productive system. The characterization of this revolutionary base does not correspond to that of other regions of the country, where historians cite displaced and marginalized social sectors.

In the state of Chihuahua, one can differentiate among at least four geographical theaters where the revolutionary response was most intense and dominant: in Parral, the district of Hidalgo; in Casas Grandes, the district of Galeana; in Chihuahua, the district of Iturbide; and in San Isidro, the district of Guerrero. In the following pages, we list a few of the characteristics of each of those districts identified as revolutionary centers.

Guerrero
In the years before the revolution, the district of Guerrero appeared in the statistical bulletins as one of the richest [of the state], with the most diversified productive activities: not only cattle ranching but also agriculture and mining. In addition, in the first years of the century, the heart of the sierra produced a forestry emporium in the community of San Pedro Madera in the municipality of Temósachic. Demographically, the district of Guerrero distinguished itself by possessing the highest number of small ranching proprietors and day laborers. This pattern suggested that agricultural property was well apportioned despite the existence of large haciendas like Palomas, Babícora, Santa Clara, San Jerónimo, and Santa Ana, among others.

On various occasions during the second half of the nineteenth century, the inhabitants of this district confronted the local authorities, and even the governor himself, Angel Trías Jr. In 1878, they launched a riot against him that led to his resignation that same year even though Trías enjoyed the full support of President Porfirio Díaz. During this period, the inhabitants of Guerrero also distinguished themselves by their participation in the campaign against the Apaches as well as various rebel uprisings against the Porfirian dictatorship.

In those years before the revolution, the tragedy of the village of Tomóchic (1891–92) still loomed large in the memory of Guerrero's inhabitants, as well as the massacre of the rebels of Temósachic and Santo Tomás in 1893. The members of the generation that took up arms in 1910—the generation of Pascual Orozco Vázquez and Marcelo Caraveo—lived the tragedy of Tomóchic up close. Many of those revolutionaries were students of the public school of the city of Guerrero when a caravan of widows and orphans reached that city late in 1892, conducted from Tomóchic by Porfirian soldiers. Thus, when the first copies of *Regeneración* arrived at the turn of the century, they avidly read the incendiary articles that Ricardo Flores Magón contributed to each issue. Later on, in 1906 and 1908, the armed uprisings organized by the Partido Liberal Mexicano produced great excitement in the region, especially because there were many family ties between the inhabitants of Guerrero and Galeana, as was the case, for example, with the Orozco family.

Speaking of Mr. Antonio Orozco, the nephew of General Pascual Orozco, two of his cousins who lived in Casas Grandes participated in the activities of the Partido Liberal Mexicano, although neither one of the two figured among the insurgents of 1910. According to don Antonio, it was through them that Pascual learned of the Magonista ideas in the pages of the newspaper *Regeneración*.[16]

In contrast to the other districts, where the revolutionary activity of 1910 remained concentrated in the primary town of each municipality, as was the case with Hidalgo, Galeana, and Iturbide, the social response was spread out in Guerrero. Contingents organized in various villages such as San Isidro, Bachíniva, Temósachic, Namiquipa, Santo Tomás, and Pachera.

Each municipality also produced capable leaders who established continuity throughout the process of the fight against the dictatorship. These men knew how to use their guns, and they had their own ideas with respect to liberty and justice. Bachíniva produced Heliodoro Olea and Luis A. García, both formed in the ideas of the Partido Liberal Mexicano; Santo Tomás brought forth José de la Luz Blanco; Pachera, Sóstenes Beltrán and Félix Terrazas; and San Isidro, Albino Frías, Marcelo Caraveo, and Pascual Orozco Vázquez. A comparison of the results of the revolutionary uprisings in the different districts of the state reveals that in Guerrero, the triumphant revolution had continuity because the social and material conditions of that region led to a popular military organization.

As a result of the war against the Apaches, and especially the campaign that took place during the years 1870–80, the inhabitants had gained experience in war and owned a large quantity of arms. During that campaign, they organized in a singular form of defense through groups of civilian volunteers who occasionally carried out campaigns of persecution against the bands of invading Indians [*sic*].

The first armed action in the district of Guerrero had as its target a small hamlet, which the revolutionaries took without any trouble on November 19; and the second aimed at the local cacique, Joaquín Chávez, who lived in San Isidro, the town from where much of the revolutionary vanguard in the district of Guerrero hailed. Later on, this revolutionary nucleus became more ambitious in its military objectives, eventually possessing enough resources to besiege and then seize Ciudad Guerrero, the municipal seat on December 2, two weeks after the first encounter. Thus we can suggest that the district of Guerrero was one of the areas in the Mexican republic that saved from failure the revolutionary movement launched by Mr. Francisco I. Madero. It produced the contingents best prepared to confront the Porfirian military.

Casas Grandes

The failure of the 1906 insurrection and the seizure of dozens of party members and a few of its important leaders did not immobilize the revolutionaries of the Partido Liberal Mexicano. Soon thereafter, they resumed their activities, concentrating their efforts in regions with a large number of readers of the newspaper *Regeneración*. That was how the young leader Práxedis Guerrero first made contact with the sympathizers from Galeana. Within a short period of time, he organized a group of several dozen men ready to take up arms at the moment of a new attempt to carry out a revolution.

The inhabitants of the Galeana district knew the ideas of the Partido Liberal Mexicano, disseminated by means of the newspaper *Regeneración*. In addition, that region was part of a geographical trail of migrant workers who periodically traveled to the mines of Arizona and New Mexico, where the Partido Liberal had managed to take root by carrying out an extensive social mobilization that wielded influence in several border towns.

A new attempt was planned for 1908. On that occasion, the revolutionaries of Galeana participated with two contingents of approximately fifty men each. The majority of these men came from the region of

Casas Grandes. Although they once again met with defeat, a defeat that resulted in several deaths and dozens of men in prison, the region later became one of the main bases of support for the Partido Liberal at the national level. To be sure, in Parral and in the state capital, there were also several dozen sympathizers.

At the moment when Francisco I. Madero made his revolutionary proclamation of November 20, the liberals of the district of Galeana led by Práxedis Guerrero relied on an army of more than one hundred men experienced in combat. They possessed a good supply of arms and ammunition, but more than anything else, that army counted on the social support of all of the towns of the district. Considering these advantages, before November 20, Práxedis Guerrero (who had become the representative of the Partido Liberal in the north of the country) concentrated the best fighters from other regions, and it was thus that César Canales, Emilio Campa, Lázaro Alanís, and others came to Chihuahua during those days.

One might recount the activities of the Partido Liberal Mexicano from 1901 until October 1910—the moment when Madero began to distribute his Plan of San Luis—and consider the role played by the newspaper *Regeneración* as a disseminator of revolutionary ideas and as a means of political organization. One might also take into consideration the effects of the strikes organized by the liberals in Cananea and Río Blanco as well as the revolutionary attempts of 1906 and 1908 on the local towns. One would then understand that the Partido Liberal Mexicano was the organization that prepared Mexicans for the insurrection, and particularly the revolutionaries of Chihuahua, who immediately placed themselves at the vanguard of this national movement.

Nonetheless, the leadership of the Partido Liberal Mexicano was not able to resolve its relationship with the Madero movement strategically, despite the affinity and participation of several Magonistas in the ranks of the army of Pascual Orozco Jr. One of the fundamental challenges in the regional historiography of this era is to elucidate the political relationship between the Orozquista contingents of the first days of the revolution and the members of the Partido Liberal Mexicano.

Beginning in 1909, the affinity between Pascual Orozco and Práxedis Guerrero became apparent, although it was not so apparent during the first days of the revolutionary movement. Práxedis Guerrero died on December 30, 1910, immediately after defeating the defenders of the village of Janos. The majority of authors have accepted the interpretation that Guerrero died in battle. Nonetheless, in 1935, Sr. Carmen Herrera published a testimonial in *El Heraldo de Chihuahua* in which he affirmed that Práxedis Guerrero fell victim to an assassination by an agent lodged in his ranks. Whatever the case, the death of Guerrero represented a loss of enormous significance for the Partido Liberal Mexicano.

Our proposal intends to signal that the movement lost its sense of strategic direction after the death of Práxedis Guerrero, during crucial days that determined the composition of the revolutionary forces. José Inés Salazar, who assumed the role of leader, did not have the same level of knowledge and contact with the direction of Ricardo Flores Magón and the other leaders of the party. Local leaders such as Luis García, José de la Luz Soto, Benjamín Aranda, Prisciliano G. Silva, or Elfego Lugo remained too isolated in their localities and with their revolutionary groups to be able to assume the functions of general leadership. With respect to Pascual Orozco, we did not find any information about his whereabouts after the assault on Palomas. In addition, the leadership of the Partido Liberal Mexicano did not know how to manage its relationship with either the principal popular armies that had formed in the revolution against Porfirio Díaz or with the ones that had formed later on in the revolution against the dictatorship of Victoriano Huerta.

Parral
During the second half of the nineteenth century, [the district of Parral] stood out for the participation of its inhabitants in various political, cultural, electoral, and mutual assistance groups. For that reason, and because of the presence of a large number of foreigners and migrants from other parts of the republic, it acquired the characteristics of an open society, receptive to new ideas and with a propensity to change. Here was founded, in 1876, the first Mutualist Society and one of the branches of the Gran Círculo de Obreros Libres de México [Great Circle of the Free Workers of Mexico]. The only Chihuahuense delegates who attended the founding meeting of the Partido Liberal Mexicano in San Luis Potosí in 1901 hailed from here. Parral also produced the Sociedad

Benjamín Franklin, which in 1878 founded an elementary school and library that still bears that name. That organization stood out because the majority of its members identified with the liberal ideas focused on cultural and social betterment.

Years later, in 1909, when the anti-reelectionists launched the call for the formation of clubs against the reelection of President Díaz, Parral witnessed great popular enthusiasm for that movement. When Francisco I. Madero visited the town in his capacity as candidate of the Partido Antirreleccionista, almost all businesses shut down to attend the meeting held at the Hidalgo monument. The occasion became a popular fiesta.

In response to the revolutionary manifesto of the Plan of San Luis, this town convoked the largest contingent of the entire state, with an army of more than four hundred men who attempted to seize the garrison on November 21. The attempt failed, and the troops dispersed to other municipalities such as Balleza, Villa Escobedo, and Santa Bárbara. After this defeat, they did not attempt a new assault on the district seat of Parral.

The explanation for this outcome lies in the lack of military experience among the insurgents as well as the absence of military chiefs capable of assuming leadership during the outbreak of the revolution. The principal chiefs of the anti-reelectionist movement in Parral were, among others, Juan Baca, Guillermo Baca, and Pedro Gómez,[17] men of high ideals and of steadfast determination but lacking military experience. For that reason, and despite the massive response of the people of Parral, the defenders of the stronghold repulsed [the rebels]. A few days later, Guillermo Baca died under mysterious circumstances.

Taking November 20 as a point of reference, and comparing the response of the people and the results obtained in the Guerrero and Hidalgo districts, one concludes the following. Despite featuring the most numerous revolutionary contingent of the state, Parral's revolutionaries met with defeat at the hands of Porfirian soldiers and volunteers. Meanwhile, the revolutionaries of Guerrero triumphed. One must also consider the fact that the revolutionaries of the district of Hidalgo, in contrast to those of Guerrero, chose one of the major cities of the state as their first target. Parral was then the second most important town, and it was protected by a large contingent of troops and volunteers who proclaimed allegiance to their *jefe politico* as well as the regime of Porfirio Díaz. In addition to the anti-reelectionist contingents that answered Madero's call in the city of Parral, revolutionary groups of Magonista tendencies also formed, directed by the brothers Elfego, José, and Jesús Lugo. These groups contributed decisively in sowing libertarian ideas [*sic*], but that movement did not succeed in consolidating itself after November 20.

Chihuahua City
Chihuahua was the geographical center and acted as the mouthpiece for all of the groups of the state, to such an extent that it featured heterogeneous political expressions as well as the political militancy and ideological formation of the principal organizers. Among those leaders, one might mention Abraham González, the head of the statewide movement, Rafael Trejo, Guadalupe Gardea, José Sáenz, and Máximo Castillo, among others, as well as leaders such as Cástulo Herrera and Silvina and Rafael Rembao who managed to set up a network of collaborators among the railroad and mine workers. In Chihuahua City, the political activity was reflected in the Club Antirreeleccionista Benito Juárez and the activism in a few factories of the city. Since the first months of 1910, *El Correo de Chihuahua* and other small newspapers such as *El Hijo del Pueblo* and *El Padre Padilla* cautiously supported the activities of the anti-reelectionists.

On November 20, the revolutionary center in Chihuahua City assumed the role of coordinating and organizing the nearby towns, while Abraham González gained recognition as the principal chief of the movement. For reasons of safety, he moved to El Paso, Texas, where he stayed during the first two months of the revolution. He rejoined the revolutionary troops in mid-February together with the contingent that accompanied Mr. Madero.

The War and Its Times
In the bibliography of the revolution, one can frequently find the assertion that this movement began in 1910 and concluded in 1916, generalizing

this timeline for the entire country. Few authors have bothered to trace the continuity of Villismo during the following four years in Chihuahua and Durango, areas that distinguished themselves as the most important social bases for the military forces of Francisco Villa. Another generalization, found especially in textbooks, consists in presenting the revolution as if it were a single block of time and a linear conflict. When the revolution is described in this way, one can understand neither how nor why differences developed between the different groups nor the military conflicts between them.

In the state of Chihuahua, the revolution of 1910 was a long process with origins that went back to 1889, principally in the old district of Guerrero. During the twenty following years, causes and reasons accumulated that surged to the surface when Francisco I. Madero launched his call for a general insurrection on November 20, 1910. On that date, an armed struggle began that did not end until ten years later, in 1920. One can distinguish four different phases in accordance with the aims of this struggle as well as the protagonists who participated in it.

The first stage can be identified strictly as "the revolution against the dictatorship of Porfirio Díaz" and is circumscribed by two dates: the beginning, on November 20, 1910, and the culmination, on May 29, 1911, with the resignation of President Díaz. One fundamental characteristic of this period is the political dominance of Francisco I. Madero, who found almost universal acceptance as the principal political leader with the exception of the members of the Partido Liberal Mexicano. On different occasions and by diverse means, the PLM partisans proclaimed that they did not recognize him as provisional president, arguing that the people rather than Mr. Madero should get to decide who would serve in that capacity.

The second phase, which one might label the Orozquista revolt, referring to General Pascual Orozco's leadership beginning in March 1912, featured the unification of the principal contingents and revolutionary chiefs from Chihuahua against Madero, from whom they officially withdrew recognition via an extensive document known as the Plan of the Empacadora, signed on April 6, 1912.[vi] That phase lasted until

vi. Vargas later gives this date as March 6, 1912. Most historical works cite March 25, which appears to be the correct date.

March 1913, when those chiefs recognized the government of Victoriano Huerta.

In his historical moment—1910–20—Pascual Orozco represented the majority opinion of the Chihuahuenses at the front. He was the incarnation of the ideas and aims of a social sector that had emerged during the revolution against the dictatorship of Porfirio Díaz. After its triumph, it lost its popular character when Madero sent home the principal chiefs and revolutionary groups, leaving in the hands of the Porfirian military the fulfillment of the objectives for which all of the Mexican people had been waiting. With respect to Castillo's participation in this phase, he himself explained how he had decided to fight against his old boss in February 1912, when he signed the Plan of the Empacadora,[vii] which listed the reasons and aims of the new revolution.[18]

The third phase began in March 1913, after Victoriano Huerta had carried out the military coup against President Madero, and concludes in September 1914, after the defeat of the Huertista dictatorship and the breakdown of the unity between Villismo and Carrancismo.

The fourth and last stage began on September 22, 1914, when the generals of the Villista División del Norte withdrew recognition from Venustiano Carranza as the chief of the Constitutionalist army, which touched off a new military confrontation between Carrancistas and Villistas. This confrontation dragged on for six years and concluded in July 1920, when Villa signed a peace agreement with the government of Adolfo de la Huerta a few months after Venustiano Carranza had fallen victim to an assassination attempt by his old military allies. One can also regard that date as marking the conclusion of the armed struggle that had begun ten years before.

Máximo Castillo, Precursor of the Revolution

By testimonial and documentary evidence dating from the time prior to November 20—including Castillo's own writings—we know that [Castillo] was one of the initiators of the revolution in 1910.[19]

He was born on a small ranch in the municipality of San Nicolás de Carretas, Chihuahua, on May 11, 1864. He experienced the author-

---

vii. Vargas is referring to the Plan of Santa Rosa (not Empacadora).

itarianism and repression of the Porfirian dictatorship from a young age.[viii] He belonged to the same generation as Albino Frías, José de la Luz Soto, José de la Luz Blanco, Félix Terrazas, Abraham González, Heliodoro Olea, Cástulo Herrera, Luis A. García, Lauro Aguirre, Pascual Orozco Sr., Seferino Pérez, and Santana Pérez, among others. They were mature men who became military chiefs of the first revolutionary groups that developed in the state of Chihuahua to combat the Díaz dictatorship, even though they had passed forty years of age by 1910. Although Castillo neither participated in the war of Tomóchic nor the rebellions of Santo Tomás, Temósachic, or Ascensión, he lived in close proximity to these events. In one way or another, the damage that the Porfirian military inflicted against the people became known all over the state. In 1881, he married María de Jesús Flores. He had only just turned seventeen, but he already knew farmwork and accepted the responsibility of founding a family along with a young woman.

During the first forty-five years of his life, Castillo traveled a long road of jobs and trades, partaking in all of the activities of poor people. At a young age, he abandoned life in the countryside and tried to improve his situation. He at first went to work in the mines and later practiced different trades until he moved to a populous working-class neighborhood in Chihuahua City, where he worked as a blacksmith. He was not well educated, but he knew how to read and write well. He spent a lot of time reflecting and worrying about the future of his fatherland, about the situation of the workers, and about the state of underdevelopment of the rural people.

Castillo painfully noted the impoverished conditions in which Mexican peons and rancheros lived, in comparison with those of the United States. He blamed the government for these conditions. Although he recognized that the government had not made him a victim, he believed that the majority of the people suffered a great deal of injustice and misery as a result of the dictatorship of General Porfirio Díaz. In 1895, he did not accept the office of mayor[ix] of San Nicolás de Carretas because

viii. In the original, "desde los primeros años de la juventud," which is misleading, given that the Porfirian dictatorship did not exert its full influence in Chihuahua until the 1880s.

ix. In the original, "presidente municipal," a word that translates better as "municipal president," the chief of a municipality. The *presidentes municipales* fulfilled the office of he thought that he could not do anything for the benefit of his fellow citizens, and that accepting this office would make him an accomplice to the government's crimes against the people. Reflecting on the situation of the Mexicans, he came to the conclusion that the government of Porfirio Díaz was responsible for their poverty and backwardness, and he was convinced that the situation needed to change.

In 1909, he began to associate with the anti-reelectionists in Chihuahua City. He made his first contacts with the anti-Porfirian struggle through the offices of his friend José Sáenz and his neighbor José de la Luz Fourzán. He relates in his memoirs that he met with Sáenz after his return from the United States. Sáenz informed him of the foundation of an anti-reelectionist club to make war against the dictator Díaz, and he invited him to join this group. Castillo responded that he did not want to because he feared going to prison, but he promised Sáenz that he would be happy to join him in firing shots if nothing had changed after the election.

A year went by, and at the end of October, Mr. José Sáenz, who had not forgotten the words of Máximo Castillo, came to see him. He explained to him that a revolutionary group was forming, and he asked him if he was ready to fulfill his promise. Castillo responded that he was indeed going to do as he had promised, and according to his memoirs, a few of the first meetings of the Chihuahuense revolutionaries took place in the forge that he owned, located in the street of José Eligio Muñoz in the Colonia Santo Niño. He explained that in early November 1910, his house became a revolutionary center where the insurgents prepared the uprising that Madero had planned for the 20th of that month. The organizer of these meetings was the railroad workers' leader, Cástulo Herrera.

A few days later, Herrera wrote a report that informed Mr. Abraham González of the preparations for the revolution. In the first part of this report, Herrera wrote that the twelve conspirators had agreed to dynamite the barracks of the Third and Twelfth Battalions at 2:00 a.m. on November 20. At the same time, they would cut off the electrical

---

mayor at the same time that they also wielded authority in the surrounding area of a town, which belonged to the same *municipio*.

lighting as well as telephone and telegraph services and imprison the leadership of the city.[20]

On approximately November 13, one week before the date announced as the beginning of the revolution, Castillo said good-bye to his family and immediately went to the northwestern region of the state, in possession of a commission to rally all of the anti-reelectionists of the small ranches in the vicinity of San Nicolás de Carretas. His effort did not meet with much success, but in any event, accompanied by his brother, Apolonio, he joined one of the armed contingents. On November 19, accompanied by Cástulo Herrera and a group of twenty revolutionaries, they encountered the revolutionary forces led by Francisco Villa in the Mena Ravine. Once these two groups had joined together, they occupied the village of San Andrés on November 21. There, they took part in a short period of fighting in which several Federal soldiers died, including a lieutenant colonel, Pablo Yepes. Forty-six years old and having left his family disconsolate, Castillo began a new phase of his life with this action. There was no return: at first, he was a Maderista, then an Orozquista, and, finally, a Zapatista.

Madero's Escort

In December 1910, Castillo joined the forces of General Orozco. On February 7, 1911, he took charge of security for a few members of Francisco I. Madero's entourage. During the following days, he participated in the maneuvers to safeguard Madero's entry into Mexican territory, which occurred on February 14, 1911. Madero came accompanied by approximately fifty North Americans and several of his closest collaborators. His brother and other members of his leadership team crossed the border several days before him in order to prepare for his arrival.

On March 6, 1911, under the military orders of Francisco I. Madero, Castillo and his soldiers participated in the attack on the fortifications of Casas Grandes. On that occasion, the Maderistas suffered one of their most tragic defeats at the hands of the Porfirian forces. Many revolutionaries and several important leaders, for example, Dolores Palomino, died during the fighting.

During the most critical moments of the battle, Mr. Madero suffered an injury to his hand. Risking his own life, Castillo took him out of harm's way, thereby saving him from dying or being taken prisoner. With this heroic act, he acquired notoriety among the troops. He also gained the support and affection of the principal Maderista bosses, and especially the Madero family, who used their influence to ensure Castillo's immediate nomination as the chief of the personal escort of the leader of the revolution. Thus, from the second week of March until the beginning of June, Castillo became the shadow of Francisco I. Madero. In his memoirs, he did not provide a detailed account of the activities in which he participated during this period. But his presence close to the chief of the revolution becomes obvious in the large number of photographs in which he appears at [Madero's] side.

After their defeat at Casas Grandes, the troops went to the Hacienda San Diego, from where they sent messages to their dispersed soldiers to return and meet up again at that place. With the exception of the group of José Inés Salazar, who went to Galeana, almost all of the dispersed troops met up again at San Diego and remained there at Madero's orders. At a meeting of his troops, Madero gave an account of the situation and encouraged his people to lift up their spirits despite the first adverse results [of the revolution]. The historian Francisco R. Almada portrays the meeting of the chief of the revolution with his troops at the Hacienda San Diego thusly:

> ... Madero was announced as provisional president of the republic,[21] in accordance with the Plan of San Luis Potosí. A bit later, a communication arrived from Pascual Orozco Jr., in which [Orozco] announced that he had arrived at the town of Galeana with a force of three hundred men. Madero and his allies went to [Galeana], and there the two revolutionary chiefs spoke for the first time.[22]

From San Diego, the revolutionaries went to the Hacienda Bustillos, where they arrived at the end of March. There, Mr. Madero, in his capacity as provisional president, signed a few decrees, also awarding the first military promotions to several revolutionary chiefs. Two weeks later, he ordered the troops to march on Casas Grandes with the objective of attacking that city once again and avenging the defeat they had suffered weeks before. While on their way, the forces received information that the Porfirians had abandoned the fortifications.

The night of April 12, the bulk of the troops arrived in Casas Grandes, and two days later, they began their march toward Ciudad Juárez. On the 15th, the Maderista advance sentinels reached the Bauche train station, where a battle took place with favorable results for the revolutionaries. A short while later, the revolutionaries set up camp in the vicinity of Ciudad Juárez.

Since before the arrival of the revolutionaries [in the vicinity of Ciudad Juárez], the Díaz government had begun negotiations. Díaz desired a peaceful solution to the conflict at all costs. But almost three weeks went by without the two sides coming to an agreement. President Díaz was ready to meet several of the demands, but he insisted on remaining in control and authority. Meanwhile, among the revolutionary camp, the conviction gradually took hold that both President Díaz and Vice President [Ramón] Corral should resign. On May 7, Díaz published a message to the Mexican people that announced that he would not resign the presidency. In response, and considering seriously the specter of U.S. military intervention under the pretext of safeguarding the inhabitants of El Paso, Texas, Madero ordered his troops to withdraw toward the southern part of the state in order to avoid an international conflict. But before that happened, on the morning of May 8, hostilities began. After two days of fighting, on May 10, the revolutionaries took the fortifications of Ciudad Juárez. According to Castillo and other authors, revolutionary contingents that disagreed with [Madero's decision] to withdraw to the south deliberately provoked the confrontation.

On May 13, 1911, three days after the revolutionary forces had defeated the Porfirians, the chiefs Pascual Orozco and Francisco Villa found themselves in conflict with Madero. They had complained to him about the lack of attention to the troops. After vainly awaiting a response, they went to the location of the provisional president with the intention of arresting him, which would have led to a conflict between those who supported Madero and those who backed Orozco and Villa. Máximo Castillo and other revolutionaries intervened and prevented the arrest and also an escalation of the incident into an armed confrontation among the revolutionaries themselves.

Historians and protagonists of this incident have each written their own version of the origin of the conflict between Madero and his principal revolutionary chiefs: Pascual Orozco and Francisco Villa. In that regard, Madero himself declared that one of the reasons for the insubordination of May 13, 1911, was the disagreement among the revolutionary chiefs regarding his nomination of a provisional cabinet in Ciudad Juárez.[23] For his part, General Marcelo Caraveo listed three causes for this confrontation in his memoirs. In general terms, he listed them as follows:

- First, the confrontation with Roque González Garza and Garibaldi. After the Battle of Ciudad Juárez, they had asked [Villa and Orozco] to hand over their weapons and ammunition: ". . . Pascual refused to give them to them because [arms and ammunition] were useless in the hands of those who had not fought."
- Second, because, according to Caraveo, Madero had promised in Ciudad Guerrero to have [the Porfirian] General Navarro sent to the firing squad. When Navarro was taken prisoner after the Battle of Ciudad Juárez, Madero himself had sent him to the North American side [of the border], thus preventing his execution.
- The third reason was that the chief of the revolution refused to heed the justified petitions of the revolutionaries to be paid, even after spending several days without even the most minimal means to live.[24]

According to the testimonials of Heliodoro Olea and Castillo himself, early that day, Pascual Orozco and Francisco Villa presented themselves [to Madero] accompanied by several of their men. They debated violently with Madero and at one point tried to arrest him. According to Máximo Castillo's story, this altercation did not get worse because he rapidly intervened, protecting the chief of the revolution with his body, thus providing a respite until cooler heads prevailed and the discussion could proceed in a peaceful manner.

In Zapatista Country

The triumph of Ciudad Juárez changed the situation rapidly in favor of the revolutionaries. The negotiations with President Díaz accelerated, and the president finally agreed to resign from office. On May 30, Francisco I. Madero commenced his triumphant journey to the capital, and at that moment, Máximo Castillo and his faithful companion Ricardo Terrazas accompanied him as those responsible for his personal escort. During this triumphant return, hundreds of last-minute revolutionary politicians also traveled alongside the new national leader, and Madero paraded along with them through the streets of the national capital on June 7.

During the following day of celebrations, the provisional president met with the revolutionary chief of the state of Morelos, Emiliano Zapata, at his family's house. After that meeting, Francisco I. Madero traveled to the state of Morelos from June 13 to 15, and Máximo Castillo was among those revolutionaries who accompanied him. In that fashion, Castillo personally got to know the agrarista ideas of Emiliano Zapata. The visit proved formative in Castillo's life. As he indicated in his memoirs, he learned there, in Morelos, the way to resolve the agrarian problem. He did not provide the exact date when this happened, but it is almost certain that it was on June 13, 1911. On the 14th, Madero traveled to Iguala and Chilpancingo and returned to Morelos two days later, on June 15 [*sic*].

Coinciding with Madero's visit, on the 13th, a meeting took place in the yard of the factory "La Carolina" where the Zapatistas delivered their weapons, receiving ten or fifteen pesos per person from the new government. According to the version that Castillo recorded in his memoirs, he was present for this act of disarming the troops of the Liberating Army of the South. Certainly, during the two following days, he visited a few villages where he witnessed firsthand the agrarian redistributions carried out directly by Emiliano Zapata. From what he was able to see and learn with regard to carrying out agrarian reform in that state, Castillo became convinced that it was the only way in which one could do justice to the landless campesinos. What he observed in Zapatista territory became the objective that, he believed, should be followed in Chihuahua as well as all of Mexico.

A few weeks after those events, in July 1911, Francisco I. Madero informed his faithful guardians, Castillo and Terrazas, that he no longer needed them because, as he said, everyone in Mexico took care of him and loved him. Thus he ordered them to return immediately to Chihuahua, where their families awaited them. Completely consternated by this decision, without any financial means, and feeling cast aside in the most decisive moments of the revolution, they began the return trip to their homeland.

During the second half of the year 1911, only a few months after the triumph of the revolution, a few towns and villages began to show signs of discontent with the electoral process. Several local revolutionary chiefs disregarded the democratic decisions of their fellow citizens and imposed their own candidates, provoking reactions of distrust and popular opposition, as well as commentaries suggesting that the same things were happening that had occurred in the age of the dictatorship. In view of this situation, Governor Abraham González commissioned Castillo to travel to some of these localities with the goal of enforcing the will of the majority. In the same way, he also got the job of combatting bands of individuals who pursued unbridled banditry. During several weeks, Castillo visited various localities along with a contingent of one hundred men, establishing order in the face of banditry and making sure that the popular will was respected in the election of their authorities.

Division in the Revolutionary Ranks

Meanwhile, in the country's capital, the principal political leaders of the revolution became mired in an electoral dispute that remained irreconcilable by means of negotiation. The motive was the substitution of the candidate for the vice presidency of the republic. In early August 1911, rumors circulated in Mexico City that Madero was preparing a new convention with the objective of changing the original candidate for the vice presidency. Representatives from several anti-reelectionist clubs met with Madero to ask him directly about his intentions. Madero replied that those rumors were unfounded. Nonetheless, after August 10, a new convention was being organized, which convinced various delegates of the old Partido Antirreleccionista that Madero was playing a two-faced game. In response, the representatives of forty anti-reelectionist clubs met and withdrew recognition from Francisco I. Madero as the head of the party.

For their part, Madero's followers attended a national convention at the end of August in which they dissolved the Partido Antirreeleccionista and replaced it with the new Partido Constitucional Progresista.

They then changed the ticket for the election, naming José María Pino Suárez as candidate for the vice presidency instead of Francisco Vázquez Gómez.[25] A large delegation from Chihuahua attended this convention, representing sixty anti-reelectionist clubs. No other state was represented with a delegation of that size, and, in fact, the vote of the Chihuahuenses proved decisive for the vote to change the slate of candidates.

When the delegates returned to Chihuahua, they faced harsh criticism because a majority of the revolutionary chiefs of the state supported the candidacy of Vázquez Gómez against that of Pino Suárez. Chihuahuenses also sent stern notes of protest to Francisco I. Madero, demanding the return to the original ticket. But these protests proved futile. These developments marked the beginning of the division of the local revolutionaries in the state of Chihuahua. From that point on, the dispute began to escalate until it erupted into open conflict by means of the Plan de la Empacadora, which began a new revolution, but this time against the government of President Francisco I. Madero.

The [substitution of the vice-presidential candidate] provoked the first political division in the ranks of the Maderistas. Although it did not have much effect in the center of the country, in the case of Chihuahua, it set off almost unanimous condemnation on the part of the revolutionaries, who considered the action by the revolutionary chief, Francisco I. Madero, a personalist and antidemocratic move. Thus began a conflict that gradually turned into an antagonistic clash.

In October 1911, just after the elections, Francisco I. Madero traveled to Chihuahua. In a rally on the Plaza Hidalgo, the new president laid out his case for replacing Vázquez Gómez. He was not very convincing, and in his frustration, he began to argue with those in attendance.

The pages of the newspaper *El Padre Padilla* dating from October 26, 1911 (no. 802), discuss this event in the following fashion:

Mr. Madero in Chihuahua
Don Francisco I. Madero arrived in this city a little after 4:00 p.m. yesterday. He received an enthusiastic and genuinely popular reception . . . The entire city took a holiday; streets and sidewalks were insufficient to contain the more than 10,000 people who filled the principal arteries of the city during the entire afternoon.

After these felicitations . . . he installed himself on the central balcony, where he heard a speech by Mr. Francisco San Martín, and then another by a young man, Fernando Aguirre . . . Aguirre praised Dr. Francisco Vázquez Gómez, which caused a very favorable impression among the immense audience. Then it was Mr. Madero's turn to speak . . . He recognized and commended the merits of don Abraham González and General Orozco . . . Mr. Madero's speech was interrupted frequently by the applause of the multitude. But where don Francisco slipped up was when he defended, at all cost, the elected vice president, the *licenciado* Pino Suárez, whom he praised effusively. The immense majority of the people responded to his words with rumbling "mueras" and prolonged hissing. Mr. Madero attacked Doctor Vázquez Gómez rudely and violently, and he almost called him a coward . . . In response to Madero's sharp attacks, the people stridently cheered the doctor every time his name was mentioned.

The president-elect said that Pino Suárez's lack of popularity only owed to the fact that his personality was not widely known, and that "the press, which had shown servility toward the dictator Díaz and had not had the civic valor necessary to confront him at the time of the revolution, had betrayed the people (upon which the people shouted: No!), creating a hostile environment for Pino." Certainly . . . Mr. Madero had forgotten that in many areas of the country, the journalists who favored the revolution suffered all kinds of attacks and difficulties, and he had also forgotten that those same journalists were the ones who had attacked and were continuing to attack Pino Suárez. To go no further, we mention here, in Chihuahua, don Silvestre Terrazas, who was imprisoned for three months because of his support of the revolutionaries. And the same Mr. Terrazas, in his newspaper, *El Correo,* is the one who has launched the most energetic campaign in this state against the defense of Mr. Madero.[26]

After this, Francisco I. Madero's last visit to Chihuahua, citizens publicly expressed their doubts and [mis]trust of the new president.

During those days, Colonel Máximo Castillo received a telegram that instructed him to once again present himself in Mexico City to take charge of the personal escort of the president of the republic. Despite the outcome of his first experience [with this task], Máximo Castillo accepted the invitation immediately and thus once again set out toward the capital of the republic in the company of Ricardo Terrazas. He believed that he would at last find himself close to the president to protect him and to observe the trajectory of the revolution from close at hand. Castillo wrote in his memoirs that when he met with President Madero, the president acted surprised and claimed that he had not solicited his presence because he did not need him. Nonetheless, he desired to offer some compensation and told him that he could give [Castillo and Terrazas] some work in Chapultepec Park, so that they could sustain themselves in light of the fact that they had already made the trip. [Castillo and Terrazas] refused to believe that the president meant what he had said, and they remained in the capital for a few weeks, hoping that he would call them back. As nothing happened, they sought to see him once again, but they were not able to obtain an audience and finally returned to Chihuahua.

Máximo Castillo, his comrades, and the revolutionaries of [Chihuahua] also waited in vain for the division of the haciendas and the fulfillment of the ideals for which they had participated in the revolution. The situation of the new government went from bad to worse, and every day that went by, the Porfirians recovered new positions in the revolutionary government, and particularly in the military. Rapidly, the president and his closest collaborators lost the authority and the mandate that the people had conferred upon them with the October 1911 vote.

Under these conditions, on November 28, 1911, the revolutionary junta of the state of Morelos, led by Emiliano Zapata, issued a document in the town of Ayala known as the Plan of Ayala.[x] This document laid out the agrarian demands ignored by President Madero, whom they accused of having violated the principles that he had vowed to defend. In his stead, they recognized General Pascual Orozco [as the head of state]. In case [General Orozco] refused to accept, they named Emiliano Zapata as the one who would assume leadership over the revolution. Among other things, that plan withdrew recognition from the Madero government for the following reasons:

> Taking into account that [he] ... left standing most of the governing powers and corrupted elements of oppression of the dictatorial government of Porfirio Díaz, ... the aforementioned Sr. Francisco I. Madero, present

x. In fact, November 27, 1911.

President of the Republic, tries to avoid the fulfillment of the promises which he made to the Nation in the Plan of San Luis Potosí; . . . [He] has tried with the brute force of bayonets to shut up and to drown in blood the pueblos who ask, solicit, or demand from him the fulfillment of the promises of the revolution, calling them bandits and rebels, condemning them to a war of extermination without conceding or granting a single one of the guarantees which reason, justice, and the law prescribe . . .[27]

Chihuahua in Rebellion

On February 2, 1912, a group of Chihuahuense revolutionaries signed the Plan of Santa Rosa, by means of which they announced their decision to take up arms against the government of Francisco I. Madero. Professor Braulio Hernández assumed the leadership of this movement. He had distinguished himself as one of the principal organizers of the 1910 revolution and had served as secretary of Governor Abraham González until a few months prior. But as one of those who had opposed the imposition of Pino Suárez, he had submitted his resignation on November 16, 1911, leaving José María Ponce de León in charge while the governor looked for a substitute. At the moment of his resignation, he told Adolfo Fuentes Gámez, a reporter and director of *El Padre Padilla*, that he found himself very disillusioned with the revolution and that he wanted to write his memoirs.[28] By all accounts, he did not fulfill this intention. On February 2, 1912, Hernández signed the Plan of Santa Rosa along with Máximo Castillo, Ricardo Terrazas, and other prestigious revolutionaries.

By means of this document, the Chihuahuenses openly expressed their opposition to the government and demanded a more radical solution to the problem of the redistribution of land. The second article among the ten that made up the plan declared the following:

We decree for reasons of public utility . . . the expropriation of the national territory with the exception of the surface occupied by urban real estate, the buildings that make up what is generally known as the *casco* of a hacienda, factory, or farm, and the lands of the railroads. The government will forever be the exclusive owner of the land and will only rent it out to all those who need it, to the extent that they can cultivate it in person and with the members of their family.[29]

The Plan of Santa Rosa did not have military consequences, but it was an unequivocal sign that President Madero had lost the support of the Chihuahuense revolutionaries by the beginning of 1912. Politically, it remained on paper and only became known in the state capital. Even though Professor Braulio Hernández had been one of the principal organizers of anti-reelectionism in 1910, by that time, he was no longer in a position of leadership.

Four weeks after the signing of the Plan of Santa Rosa, at the beginning of March, the revolutionary chiefs of the Ejército Libertador del Norte rebelled against President Madero. They met in Chihuahua City on March 6 with the objective of signing a new plan, which became known as the Plan of the Empacadora because it was signed in a place in the periphery of the city very close to an old meatpacking plant. Those present included Pascual Orozco, José Inés Salazar, Emilio Campa, Lázaro Alanís, Rodrigo Quevedo, Professor Braulio Hernández, and Máximo Castillo, among many other revolutionary leaders who had distinguished themselves in the fight against the military forces of Porfirio Díaz. Among the signatories of the Plan of the Empacadora, we also find several revolutionaries from the Galeana district who were old comrades of the Magonista leader, Práxedis Guerrero. They contributed significantly to the writing of the plan. For that reason, one can affirm that the Plan of the Empacadora was derived from the Magonista program. The movement spread rapidly, when the principal revolutionary contingents from the state of Chihuahua joined. After a few weeks, it acquired regional character by incorporating groups from Sonora, Durango, and Coahuila.

Although the leaders present in Ciudad Juárez[xi] initiated this movement, General Pascual Orozco joined it later on, and for that reason, the press identified the members of this movement as "Orozquistas" and also as "Reds," an adjective that had been used only months before to identify the Magonistas. In response, the defenders of the government of Francisco I. Madero touched off an intense and libelous press campaign in which they decried General Pascual Orozco as a traitor who

---

xi. Occupied during the first days of the rebellion, Ciudad Juárez became the capital of the rebel movement.

had sold out his conscience to the landowning elite that was an enemy of the revolution.

Orozquistas and Huertistas

On March 23, 1912, the two armies clashed for the first time in the vicinity of Rellano Station, a point located between Jiménez and Escalón in the south of the state of Chihuahua. It was an important battle to which the government of President Madero had committed itself fully, using its best contingents, directed personally by the secretary of war, General José González Salas. For many reasons, the Battle of Rellano impacted national opinion and especially the inhabitants of the state of Chihuahua, who had never before seen on their fields two armies so numerous (according to the historian Michael C. Meyer, six thousand soldiers on each side).[30]

In those moments, the prevailing opinion was that if the Orozquista forces triumphed, they would no longer face any obstacle until reaching the capital of the republic, and thus it was thought that Madero's tenure in the presidency depended on a triumph in Rellano. That was what the secretary of war, General José González Salas, believed, who put himself at the command of the federal forces.

The most intense part of the combat took place during March 24 and 25, which concluded with the defeat of the Federal forces. According to Michael Meyer, five hundred soldiers died on the battlefield between the two sides, but mostly among the Federals. General González Salas felt responsible for the failure and, anticipating the consequences of the defeat, locked himself in his railroad wagon and shot a bullet into his brain.

In his place, President Madero gave the command of his troops to General Victoriano Huerta, who came from Mexico City to reorganize the Federal army now stationed in Torreón, Coahuila. In the course of three months, from April to June 1912, Huerta directed a successful campaign, defeating the Orozquistas several times and managing to destroy the bulk of the rebel army.

In late 1912, the situation of the Orozquistas was disastrous. Instead of fighting, they ambulated from one side to another avoiding the encounter with the Huertista troops. General Orozco had lost control of the situation. We can say of his troops that they were dispersed contingents rather than an army, each subsisting as they could, without ammunition and without the financial resources to buy food, not to mention clothing. One can suggest that General Huerta deliberately avoided annihilating them, letting this movement survive, and thus maintaining the possibility of an alliance in the future.

During the last months of 1912, the military and logistical conditions of the Orozquistas became very difficult, and the contingents that most acutely felt these difficulties were those most disconnected from the central army. Such was the case with the contingent of Máximo Castillo, who by the beginning of 1913 had become very disillusioned with Pascual Orozco and other chiefs such as José Inés Salazar. He criticized them for the way in which they had conducted several battles.

At the end of the year, the prestige and leadership of Huerta among the Porfirian military leaders had been consolidated, and the old generals began to prepare for the propitious moment for their return to power. In another sense, the position of President Madero weakened rapidly due to his own errors and because of the large number of enemies of the revolution who had ensconced themselves in the principal positions of the army and the government. At the beginning of 1913, several conspirators secretly prepared to participate in a final coup against the Madero presidency. According to various authors such as Alfonso Taracena, one of the conspirators against the government was Venustiano Carranza, who supposedly had an agreement with the [old Porfirian] General Bernardo Reyes.[31]

But among all the conspirators, the strongest one was the chief of the army, General Victoriano Huerta, who decided to deliver the coup de grace by setting in motion the military machinery against the constitutional government. The moment arrived on February 13, 1913. On that day, the military uprising began that concluded on February 22 with the assassination of President Madero and Vice President Pino Suárez.

The popular response against the authors of the coup was not immediate. During the first weeks, the new government took power without any problems. By the end of February, the majority of the governors had expressed their recognition of President Victoriano Huerta, and on

March 2, the new government celebrated an homage to the members of the army and the "defenders" of the Mexico City army who had behaved "heroically." On March 4, [however], the governor of Sonora, Ignacio Pesqueira, withdrew recognition from Huerta. On the 6th of that same month, Chihuahua governor Abraham González was assassinated. On the 11th, Venustiano Carranza declared his opposition to the Huerta government in a letter responding to the proposals that Huerta had sent to him on February 27 with the objective of gaining Carranza's recognition of his government.

Three weeks after Madero's assassination, on March 13, one of Huerta's objectives met with success when the principal Orozquista leaders accepted the alliance that he had offered them. That day, Victoriano Huerta and Pascual Orozco embraced. Also present were the following leaders: Benjamín Argumedo, Cheché Campos, Marcelo Caraveo, José Córdoba, Félix Terrazas, Damián Rodríguez, Ricardo Gómez Robelo, and others of his most loyal comrades. In exchange, Huerta agreed to comply with a list of seven demands that [Orozco] had submitted to him as conditions. The seven points of this accord between Pascual Orozco Jr. and the representatives of General Victoriano Huerta were the following:

I. The government of General Huerta would promise to resolve as soon as possible the agrarian problem in the state of Chihuahua, acquiring land appropriate for agriculture for the purpose of dividing this land among farmers of revolutionary origin via the payment of a price under easy conditions, under the condition that [those farmers] could neither sell nor mortgage their land.

II. The Orozquista soldiers who had left the rebel ranks for political reasons would be reinstated, and they would receive preference for public offices.

III. Recognition of the military ranks awarded by the chief of the rebellion, as well as guaranteed payment for the personal effects of those who had left his service, subject to the return of the equipment that they had in their possession.

IV. The government of General Huerta would pay the debts incurred by the Orozquista Rebellion as well as indemnities to the revolutionaries for the expenses that they might have incurred during their participation in the movement, by means of immediate payment of an amount equivalent to 10–20 percent and the rest a short while later.

V. Assign and pay pensions to the widows and orphans of the revolution.

VI. The Orozquista Rebellion would be represented in the cabinet of General Huerta by the engineer and general David de la Fuente as secretary of communications and public works and by the *licenciado* Manuel Garza Aldape, as secretary of agriculture, immediately after the formation of that agency.

VII. Generals Orozco Jr., Salazar, Argumedo, Caraveo, and Campa would be obligated to offer their cooperation in the work of pacification of the republic.[32]

That was how the Chihuahuense revolutionaries, the chiefs and contingents most identified with Orozco and including several Magonistas, linked their fate to that of the new dictator. With this action, they went to the other shore of the revolutionary movement and of history. The military coup and the enthroning of Victoriano Huerta in the presidency drove the Orozquistas toward a crossroads to which they failed to respond in the best manner. Just a year before, they had declared war on President Madero and accused him of having betrayed the revolutionary ideals. Huerta had defeated them and was the reason for the failure of the Plan of the Empacadora. Nonetheless, at this moment, they accepted an alliance with his government, assuming before the people a measure of complicity in the military coup.

In contrast to Orozco, Emiliano Zapata did not accept the alliance with Huerta and declared war on him after a few days. Meanwhile, Venustiano Carranza made himself first chief of the Constitutionalist army and the main protagonist of a plan signed on March 26, 1913, in the Hacienda Guadalupe in the state of Coahuila, which also declared war on Victoriano Huerta's government.

The Zapatista of the North

Máximo Castillo broke with his old Orozquista friends after they recognized the Huerta regime. But he did not join the Constitutionalist movement; instead, he assumed an independent position. On another front, on March 26, 1913, Francisco Villa crossed the border between the United States and Chihuahua accompanied by a number of followers. A few days before, the troops of Manuel Chao and Maclovio Herrera, who in 1912 had passed over to the Federal army along with their contingents, had risen up in arms. As irregular [battalions], they had participated in the defense of Madero's government during the Orozquista Rebellion.

When General Victoriano Huerta assumed the presidency of the republic by military coup, Chao, Herrera, the Rodríguezes, and other midlevel leaders from the south of the state abandoned the Federal army and became the first in Chihuahua who fought against the new regime. Months later, they joined their forces to those of Francisco Villa, whom they recognized as chief, and formed the new División del Norte, which created what has historically become known as Villismo.

Also in March 1913, Castillo met in El Paso with the licenciado Emilio Vázquez Gómez, a national representative of the Zapatista movement. The two agreed to fight in the north for the ideals of the Plan of Ayala, and Castillo received a promotion to the rank of brigadier general.[33] Following up, Castillo sent a letter to General Emiliano Zapata informing him that the revolution in the north had not ended and that he, with a group of followers, would continue the fight and awaited [Zapata's] instructions.

According to his memoirs, on April 24, 1913, Castillo announced a manifesto to the nation that identified the principles of his movement, outlined his position vis-à-vis the Orozquistas, and defined his own revolutionary objectives. These objectives were fundamentally *agrarista*. He also called upon the true revolutionaries to proclaim allegiance to the Plan of Ayala.

During the first days of June 1913, Máximo Castillo carried out agrarian reform on several haciendas owned by Luis Terrazas.[34] Aware of the fact that Francisco Villa was close to Casas Grandes, he wrote him a letter proposing his alliance with his movement. But there was no reply, and the letter remained unanswered.

A little later, the reply came by other means. Close to Casas Grandes, Villa surprised one of Castillo's groups led by José and Francisco Parra. After a brief combat, [Castillo's men] were defeated and the two chiefs executed, even though they had surrendered and had been taken prisoner. With that action, it became clear that Villa had no intention of allying with Máximo Castillo, the chief of the Zapatistas in Chihuahua.

Although several hundred revolutionaries accepted the leadership of Máximo Castillo, the contingent that accompanied him barely passed the number fifty, and that explains the difficulties that they confronted for their own maintenance. A comparison of the organization and discipline of this army with that then being organized by Francisco Villa makes Castillo's disadvantage obvious.

After the first confrontations with the Villista forces, many of the Chihuahuense Zapatistas began to desert, retiring to their homes or joining the Villista forces. In their view, there was no reason to keep fighting since the principal enemy was the government of Victoriano Huerta. Everything else appeared secondary. Along with the lack of resources, this reasoning constituted the principal impediment to Castillo and his Zapatista movement.[35]

After several weeks, and while Villa's army kept growing, Castillo's army dispersed, leaving him with very few soldiers. His agrarian redistributions were diluted because the beneficiaries had no military protection. The occupants found themselves facing the specter of their violent dislodgment by Villista troops, since Villa considered them his enemies. In his strategy, there was no room for land reform until the definitive triumph of the revolution was guaranteed. On August 12, 1913, the press in Chihuahua informed the public that Máximo Castillo had surrendered for the third time. They also wrote of his defeat between Pearson and Casas Grandes, and that he faced pursuit by both government and Villista forces.[36]

With respect to the relationship between Villa and Castillo, one finds a very curious document in the archive of the Secretaría de Relaciones Exteriores [the Mexican foreign ministry]. On September 26, 1913, the inspector of the Servicio Consular Mexicano sent a message from

El Paso, Texas, to the ministry in Mexico City, informing his superiors that he had left that day to go to Palomas, Chihuahua, accompanied by "Colonel" Enrique Portillo and Captain Miranda. The goal was to pursue the "bandit" Pancho Villa, as [the inspector] had received information from Juan Vázquez, the chief of arms of Ciudad Juárez, in the sense that Villa was injured and had become the prisoner of Máximo Castillo. The intention of the inspector, as becomes clear in the aforementioned document, was to convince Castillo of the necessity of executing Villa as soon as possible.[37]

The next day, this same inspector, whom we only know by his last name, Diebold, informed [his superiors] that he had found out that his information was incorrect, based on his investigation in Palomas. He added that the bandit Castillo had abandoned his encampment in Palomas one week prior, leaving in the direction of Ascensión accompanied by sixty people.

Pearson and the Railroad of the Northwest

At the beginning of the year 1914, Castillo found himself virtually defeated, and he could count on the support of only a few dozen men. That is how he describes it in his memoirs, where he outlines his situation, recognizing that he had retreated to the defensive, pursued by Villistas and Carrancistas, whom he could not engage in battle because his troops were reduced in number. In his memoirs, he relates how he sent Colonel Manuel Gutiérrez and Lieutenant Tomás Pérez on a commission to the Valle de San Buenaventura. After they had taken that village, they were defeated the very next day. He adds that on February 12, a large enemy contingent surprised him, and that after this defeat, he decided to move toward El Paso, where he had a group of approximately one hundred followers who were ready to join his ranks, and who had not yet already done so only because they needed money for their mobilization.

In the end, the Zapatista movement directed by Máximo Castillo could only sustain itself for six months in precarious conditions. Its geographical reach was reduced to the area of Madera, Casas Grandes, and Galeana. It never managed to expand to other regions of the state. In the pages of his memoirs, the general writes nothing about this state of affairs, but one can surmise that it was the main reason for his failure.

The region of Casas Grandes and Galeana, where Castillo decided to construct his social base, boasted a long revolutionary tradition because it had been the place where the first Magonista revolutionary groups had organized beginning in 1906. From there emerged leaders and contingents who distinguished themselves in the most difficult moments of 1910 and 1912. Nevertheless, by mid-1913, few neighbors were ready to ally themselves with General Máximo Castillo's movement.

The Pearson railroad station was a strategic point because there was much activity there, since it was the place of transit for large quantities of wood and minerals. In addition, it was the regional headquarters of the Ferrocarril del Noroeste (Railroad of the Northwest), as well as the location of a large store that supplied the inhabitants of the region with provisions and wares. Certainly, Castillo had counted on being able to obtain resources from the railroad to meet the expenses of his troops, but he did not meet his objective and soon found himself without the means to sustain his small army.

When Castillo selected the Pearson region as his base of operations, he did not know that Villa had made a deal with the railroad company that guaranteed it protection and security. Based on this accord, the directors of the railroad were in constant communication with Villa, who fully assumed the rule pursuing the "bandits" who impeded the free transit of the engines. One can suggest that the existence of this deal with the railroad company was one of the reasons why Villa could not accept the alliance that Castillo offered him. Moreover, it is possible that Villa did not take Castillo seriously because a realistic look at the political landscape convinced him that [Castillo] had no possibilities for growth since it was the fight against the murderer Huerta that was mobilizing the revolutionaries from Chihuahua and the entire country at that moment.

There is some documentary evidence of the conflict between Máximo Castillo and the company preserved in the correspondence of the Ferrocarril del Noroeste de México, an archive kept in the [Nettie Lee] Benson Collection of the University of Texas. We consulted the corresponding documents from the period July 1912 to February 1914 and found several letters in which the railroad employees informed their superiors in New York about the problems that they experienced with

Máximo Castillo and his troops. Among other things, they claimed that [Castillo] constantly demanded money from the company, blackmailing them with the threat of blowing up bridges or large sections of railroad track.

For example, on May 19, 1913, an employee reported that when Castillo's people moved to the north of Casas Grandes, they burned eight bridges close to Corralitos and demanded the immediate payment of two thousand pesos in exchange for protecting the railroad lines during the month of May. Mr. J. C. Hayes, the author of this message, explained that they had decided not to pay anything to Castillo and to pursue him with people paid by the company. Another message from June 2, signed by J. O. Crockett, informed the company that Castillo's forces had detained two southbound cargo trains in Guzmán and threatened to dynamite the trains unless the company paid ten thousand pesos in cash before 10:00 p.m., as well as US$1.25 for each head of cattle transported in the wagons. On June 10, the same J. O. Crockett let it be known that the rebels had taken Pearson after a battle of twelve hours and that they had captured 185 Federal soldiers before demanding a high sum under threat of burning down the station if their requirements were not met. On June 23, Crockett informed his superiors that Francisco Villa had arrived at Casas Grandes and then at Pearson with his troops, where they executed three suspects, threatening to hang Castillo himself as soon as they could get their hands on him. Crockett added that Villa brought 1,100 soldiers and had another 800 in Villa Ahumada as well as 1,200 in Ciudad Juárez. On July 21, Crockett wrote that Villa's forces had defeated Castillo's in Casas Grandes, killing eight and capturing twelve including Colonel Parra and his son, both executed right then and there. Crockett's message indicated that "a mass of Villa's men killed eight and captured twelve of Castillo's men in Casas Grandes in combat waged on the 12th. Colonel Parra and his son, both serving the rebels, were killed."

One of these documents offers information by means of which one can understand the sentiment of Mexicans vis-à-vis U.S. citizens. In a message signed by J. M. Peck on September 6, 1913, the author complained about the constant acts of theft committed by the inhabitants and signaled that small children were more problematic than adults because they broke windows and threw stones at the mills making use of their slingshots. He concluded with the following declaration: "There is considerable resentment among the peons against the Americans, and the best policy right now is to employ few Mexicans. The great majority of the people here sympathize with those of the red flag." On December 17, J. O. Crockett sent a memorandum to his chief, H. I. Miller of the Central of New York, indicating that thirty-three of the thirty-five bridges burned by Castillo's men had been repaired; that Francisco Villa had promised ample protection; and that one hundred Villista men had left Ciudad Juárez the preceding week who had attacked Castillo in Palomas, killing six and injuring ten others.

A reading of this voluminous collection of telegrams sent from Pearson to New York reveals that the railroad employees constantly informed their superiors about the destruction of bridges and tracks, blaming Castillo's men for these heinous acts. According to these telegrams, these men insisted on extorting large sums of money and the delivery of grains and all kinds of goods from Pearson's store. The employees reported to their bosses their rejection of these demands, and then they informed them that in response, the rebels devastated the tracks time and again. The repairs cost a lot of money, and the company's books reflected great expenses for that purpose. Who was there to prove all that the employees alleged? Who could verify that so many bridges and tracks were indeed destroyed? How could the directors in New York know that the company needed to spend thousands of pesos every month in the repair of these bridges and tracks? There is no way to know. It seems strange, if not incredible, that Castillo's men used the destruction of the railroad as their only form of pressure, and that they would not have thought to sack the great store of Pearson, where they could have found abundant quantities of all the supplies that they needed. The way the railroad employees wrote their reports, from Chihuahua to New York, the events of the second half of the year 1913, and also the way they described the explosion of the Cumbre Tunnel make one think that they were not sticking strictly to the truth. Instead, they attributed to Máximo Castillo and his men fault and responsibility without any more evidence than their own assertions, concocted most of the time to serve their own ends.

However one sees these events, one can appreciate that Castillo's actions in those months were those of a desperate man. He was the leader of a movement without a future, without possibilities of development in the state, and even less so in the area that he had chosen as his base of social support.

The Disaster of the Cumbre Tunnel

At the end of January 1914, Castillo's situation could not have been any more dramatic. He was alone, without food, ammunition, or money. Manuel Gutiérrez, his most faithful ally, still had several dozen men under his command, and although he accepted [Castillo's] authority, he really acted independently and according to the few options left to him due to his persecution by Villa's troops.

On February 4, 1914, two trains collided inside the Cumbre Tunnel, located at kilometer 347 of the Ferrocarril del Noroeste de México line, between the villages of Madera and Pearson. The following day, the reports of the railroad employees and the United States press provided an account of the catastrophe, placing blame right away on Máximo Castillo as the responsible party. Looking at the accounts from the newspapers as well as the railroad employees, one can reconstruct this event in the following fashion.

That day, a group of armed men detained a cargo train with a large number of empty cages used for cattle transport in the Cumbre Tunnel. They then forced the crew to put the engine in reverse, separating the cages. After leaving them in the tunnel, they set them on fire, and the flames rapidly spread to the wooden beams of the tunnel itself. Thereafter, they quickly started the two engines that pulled the train, and those went off track in a place where [the men] had previously removed the rails, from where they fell to the bottom of the ravine and were destroyed completely. In light of what had happened, the crew asked for permission to inform the passenger train of the same company that had followed the empty train south and that was supposed to arrive at the tunnel in a few moments. The assailants resolutely refused this request and made the crew continue on its way south on foot. For their part, the robbers continued in the opposite direction. A few moments later, the passenger train entered the tunnel, which was full of smoke. Since the crew [of that train] was unable to see what lay ahead, the train collided with the empty cars. The impact was tremendous; the engine went off track and was trapped between the fire and a tangled mess of iron. All of that made impossible any return maneuver that would have extracted the passenger train from the tunnel, which had a length of one kilometer. The exact number of passengers who lost their lives in the catastrophe remains unknown, but from available data, one can estimate that approximately seventy victims perished—men, women, and children.

On the following day, the directors of the company in New York received a message informing them that Castillo and his men had been those responsible for the collision of the passenger train running from south to north with several cars that had been set on fire after lodging them inside the Cumbre Tunnel. The message went on to say that a rescue operation had been under way since the day of the disaster that included experts from the Phelps-Dodge company, but that the number of victims and the extent of damage to the tunnel remained unknown. This notice reached even the government in Washington. J. O. Crockett, the vice president of the railroad company, solicited the intervention of his government because, as he believed, the rebels had taken the passengers prisoner, even though the inhabitants of Madera had reported that all of the crew and passengers in the train had died. In that same message sent on February 7, Crockett affirmed that approximately six hundred Villistas had arrived in the area with the intention of pursuing Castillo and his companions. In a separate communication, the Madera employees informed the company that General Villa was extremely upset about the damage caused by Castillo, and that he had sent four hundred cavalrymen with strict orders not to return until finding and arresting him.

All of the reports exchanged between the employees of the railroad company as well as all of the press coverage coincided in assigning full responsibility to Castillo and his people. For his part, Castillo steadfastly denied his involvement, as evidenced in the newspapers of the era as well as his memoirs. According to what Castillo wrote in his memoirs, he was far away from the location on the day of the disaster and unaware of what had happened, because his primary preoccupation during those weeks had been to find refuge on the other side of the [international] border. He found himself subjected to intense persecution. His memoirs capture those moments. He writes that he had gone on the defensive a while before because large groups of Villistas and Carrancistas pursued him, and because he only had a few people remaining with him. As he wrote, in early February, Colonel Manuel Gutiérrez and Lieutenant Tomás Pérez had left his column and gone somewhere else. He later made reference to the fact that a large enemy contingent had surprised him on February 12, and that all of his people had taken flight in different directions. All lost their horses and provisions. On the 13th, on foot and without food, he had consulted with his six remaining companions about the situation, and they had agreed to go to El Paso to see if it would be possible to raise one hundred men who had desired to join his movement a while ago, but who had not entered Mexico because of a lack of funds to travel to Columbus, New Mexico, from where they could cross over. As he reports, at that moment, the movement had two thousands pesos remaining, and they thought that this amount would be sufficient to pay the train fare for the people whom they counted on in U.S. territory. Historian Francisco R. Almada described this moment thus:

> Colonel Encarnación Salcedo pursued and defeated Castillo in December 1913. His forces once again caught up with him in Casas Grandes, where eight of his troops died, and six fell prisoners. He also lost thirty horses and fifty guns. In Palomas, [Castillo] had a third unfavorable encounter with Majors Primo Salcido and Miguel Samaniego, after which he could no longer sustain himself and emigrated to the United States. Only Manuel Gutiérrez remained at the head of a small band of "Castillistas" in the western region of the Galeana district, and it was he who provoked the crash of the mixed train on the way from Madera to Casas Grandes with the objective of destroying the Cumbre Tunnel. Between the crew and passengers, forty-two people died in this accident.[38]

Thus, they finally decided to cross the border with the purpose of finding new support among the exiles who sympathized with their cause.

They no longer had any other alternative. The incipient Zapatista movement in Chihuahua found itself annihilated in military terms, without soldiers, without money, and without any possibility of recovering their positions. That army of five hundred men that had begun the revolution months before under the banner of the Plan of Ayala had disbanded. The majority had deserted, and by the middle of February, only Castillo and six companions remained: four men and two women.

Castillo Is Imprisoned in the United States

On February 16, 1914, shielded by the darkness, Castillo and his men crossed the borderline. When he set foot on U.S. territory, border guards were already waiting for him. They had received information from Villista spies who had learned of the intentions of Castillo and his companions.

The press of El Paso, Texas, kept [its readership] constantly abreast of all news regarding the search [for Castillo]. Among other things, it reported that the troops of General Villa were in close pursuit of the chief of the bandits, Máximo Castillo, in order to avenge the Cumbre Tunnel disaster. [According to the press, Castillo] had taken up refuge at the border along with a small group of women and men.

On February 17, [the press] announced the capture, characterizing Castillo as the boss of the bandits who had caused the Cumbre disaster. The account stated that he had been captured on the afternoon of the preceding day on the North American side of the border, in Alamo Hueco, close to Hachita, New Mexico, with six followers. The press reported that Thomas A. Rothwell from the Ninth Cavalry of the United States had awaited him there because he had received information during the prior day about a bandit in the vicinity, and that [Castillo] had surrendered without the slightest resistance. It was anticipated that they would probably be imprisoned in Fort Bliss until the government decided whether to deliver him to General Villa, who had threatened to kill them if he captured them himself.

The capture and presentation of Máximo Castillo gave rise to much sensationalism. The newspaper and newsreel reporters played the situation to the hilt and photographed and filmed [the subjects]. A large throng congregated to meet the "heartless assassin," the "most dangerous Mexican criminal" responsible for an assault that had claimed many North American lives. Castillo and his companions were a sensation, the criminals of the moment.

On February 19, 1914, the *El Paso Morning Times* reported that a multitude awaited the arrival of Máximo Castillo at the station, and that precautionary measures would be taken to avoid acts of revenge and retaliation at the moment of his arrival. The reporter speculated in his article about the possibility of an assassination attempt at the hands of a friend or relative of one of the victims of the tunnel disaster. He added that [the authorities] had awaited Castillo's arrival since the night of the 18th,[xii] and that more than one hundred North Americans had gathered since then who had suffered greatly at the hands of the bandit chief and his minions. Some of them commented that it would not be a crime to "snuff out" the life of that man before giving General Villa the opportunity to do so.

The same article included Villa's response to the reporter when he asked him what he had in mind for the moment when he had Castillo and his companions in his hands. According to the *El Paso Morning Times,* Villa replied as follows:

You should publish in capital letters . . . and send to the newspapers from all over the world the following: if the North American authorities do not mete out adequate punishment for Máximo Castillo and his gang for the crimes of Cumbre, then they should deliver them to me so that I can execute them publicly, as I have already stated. You may invite the readers from all over the world to be present for the act.

Of course, they will face a trial, but the proof against them is overwhelming. Their deaths will be worthy of piety, but they will be violent. They will not be tortured, but they will pay for their crimes with their lives. I say it and I mean it. I fear that the North American authorities will not find a legal means to deliver Castillo to me unless the immigration authorities decide to deport him as an undesirable foreigner. For me, that is my only hope as my attorneys have informed me.

I hope that the immigration authorities will expel them, and I will take care of the rest. If that happens, the North American public should

xii. This timeline does not compute as per the rest of the chronology presented in this section.

not feel sorry when it comes to the punishment of Castillo and his collaborators. The horrible death of innocent civilians in the Cumbre disaster must be avenged.[39]

According to the newspapers, General Castillo arrived at El Paso on February 19, two days after being captured. Another article in the *El Paso Morning Times* from February 20 describes Castillo's reception not as that of a criminal but rather as a demonstration of solidarity on the part of thousands of Mexicans who had found refuge [from the fighting] beginning several months ago. For example, the newspaper announced that "saluted by a multitude estimated at ten thousand people," Máximo Castillo and six members of his gang had been captured and taken to El Paso; that they had been taken to the guard house in Fort Bliss that same afternoon, which made them fellow prisoners of General Inés Salazar; that two great army processions had awaited the bandits; that Castillo and his six companions "had been virtually pulled into the inside of the trucks by black soldiers, so that they could then be speedily taken across the city in the direction of Fort Bliss." As regards [Castillo's] replies, the commentary was to the effect that they were monosyllabic, as he confined himself to saying only "yes" or "no." The only exception occurred when he was asked about the disaster of the Cumbre Tunnel, where fifty-five Mexicans and North Americans had lost their lives. In that moment, his "wolf-like eyes had emitted sparks," and he had shouted loudly, lifting his hands in a dramatic gesture:

That is not true. I have never killed a single man, except in self-defense. Charging me with the destruction of the Cumbre Tunnel and the loss of all of these innocent lives is nothing more than another demonstration of the ways in which my enemies try to demonize me. I did not set fire to the train in the Cumbre Tunnel. I don't know anything about the accident, and I don't have anything to do with it. It was Villa's men who blew up this tunnel to sack the train, and they never thought that their action would have this result. I am innocent, and if they shoot me tomorrow, I will swear that this is the truth.[40]

The same newspaper included Castillo's reply to a question from a reporter about the cause for which he was fighting. Castillo responded that the fight was "for justice, liberty, and the land that Francisco I.

Madero had promised." He said that he had once believed in Pascual Orozco, who had turned his back on the poor and joined the traitor Huerta. He added that he knew then that they could not expect anything from the people they had trusted, and that only a few trusted wards had followed him to the western part of Chihuahua, which had been home to them until before Madero touched off the revolution. That was why they decided to take some land from the foreign invaders so they and their children would have work.[xiii]

Another press article reported that Castillo had been interned in Fort Bliss with his hands tied behind his back and his straw sombrero almost at the level of his eyebrows to avoid being burned by the sun. The article went on to state that his growing beard and disheveled hair made him seem like the grandfather of the handsome captain of the presidential guard who had commanded Madero's mounted troops after his victory at Juárez.

At the time of Máximo Castillo's capture, Fort Bliss had been converted into a gigantic concentration camp that held thousands of Mexican soldiers as if in a corral. A part of these troops had belonged to the Huertista army under the command of General Salvador Mercado; and another, to the forces of Pascual Orozco, who had been defeated at Ojinaga by Francisco Villa's forces on January 10, 1914. That day, after their defeat, the Huertista-Orozquista soldiers crossed the river and entered the territory of the United States, where North American soldiers awaited them, taking them to Fort Wingate and Fort Bliss. The El Paso press reported their number as 8,180, including 1,250 women and 556 children. Of the latter, 400 were of school age. The press also reported 53 Federal officers wounded as well as 187 troops.[41]

After the interrogation and his exhibition as the bloodiest wild beast, Máximo Castillo was taken to Fort Bliss, where he shared a cell with José I. Salazar. Thanks to this fact, one can learn from his memoirs the conditions in which they remained prisoners during those months. The José Inés Salazar whom Castillo depicts by means of his commentary seems like a person whom we do not know well. He appears as

---

xiii. Note the contradiction from the analysis above, which identified the Mexican landlord Luis Terrazas—and not North American landowners—as the target of Castillo's agrarian redistributions.

a vacillating man, surprised by the consequences of his participation alongside Victoriano Huerta's government as well as by the results that the revolution had yielded up to the moment. After a few months, Salazar left Fort Bliss; a few years later, in 1916, when he was a prisoner in the penitentiary in Chihuahua City, he was freed by Francisco Villa and joined his forces, distinguishing himself as one of the few Magonistas who allied with Villa. General Castillo remained in Fort Bliss until May 4, 1914, when he was taken to Fort Wingate, in New Mexico, where he stayed for a while. Everything appears to indicate that he later returned to Fort Bliss, where he lived until his release.

The Cumbre Tunnel catastrophe seems very strange, because at a distance, it appears as an inexplicable, purposeless act. During all of the time during which Castillo participated in the revolutionary movement, he never gave the impression of one acting in an impulsive or impetuous manner. To the contrary, he distinguished himself as a person of reasonable temperament, and as a sensible man.

Considering the conditions in which Castillo found himself during those days, almost alone and on the run, we do not see any reason why he would have given the orders to blow up the train. The only possible explanation could be that he had done it to avenge the company's owners' refusal to give him the money that he demanded, but that would have happened at another point in time, not when he was close to an obvious defeat. Ninety years after the disaster of the Cumbre Tunnel, the responsible party for this catastrophe still remains a mystery. When the North American [authorities] interrogated Castillo, he affirmed that the fault lay with Francisco Villa's men. But that explanation, too, seems faulty because at that time, Villa's relationship with the North Americans was excellent.

According to Castillo's account in his memoirs, the United States authorities finally recognized that he was innocent of the charges levied against him as regarded the explosion of the train in the Cumbre Tunnel. That is where the most controversial part of this issue comes into play. It is very clear that the North Americans gathered the necessary information to arrive at that conclusion; otherwise, they would never have released him, and they would also have known how the accident took place. Nevertheless, the press of the period never rendered a final judgment.[42]

As a result, other questions come to the surface. What happened to Castillo's troops who accompanied him at the moment of his capture? Who were they, and since when had they formed a part of his army? Why did the North Americans decide to take Castillo to Havana? We do not know the answers, and neither do we know the conditions in which he lived during the last years of his life. Nevertheless, one should not discount the hypothesis that the government of the United States made the decision to apprehend Castillo—just like the death of Orozco or the capture and death of Ricardo Flores Magón—for its own convenience or due to their agreement with their Mexican allies of the moment. One should not forget that, according to the press, the capture took place based on information provided by General Francisco Villa's spies, who demonstrated great interest in taking charge of the situation, demanding the extradition of the prisoners in order to punish them. There is also the fact that in 1914, the principal ally of the United States was General Francisco Villa, and that the agrarian project that Castillo had promoted since 1913 was neither convenient for the United States nor for General Villa's plans.

In the last months of 1914, the position of the North American government with respect to the Villista forces changed radically. For the North American government, Francisco Villa was no longer the most convenient ally, which was a determining factor in the liberation of Máximo Castillo. But on the other hand, the North American government also did not want to be responsible in case Villa assassinated General Castillo.

This hypothesis coincides squarely with Castillo's account in his memoirs. First, he was accused of having violated the territorial laws of that nation; then he was blamed for the catastrophe of Cumbre Tunnel; and at the end of his account, he relates how a North American immigration inspector notified him that he was being held prisoner for having entered the country illegally, recognizing in his presence that the accusation of the explosion of the train in Cumbre was unjustified. The inspector told him that he would not be a prisoner if he had asked for permission to enter the territory of the United States. He also told him that the intention of the North American government was to set him free, but that it feared that General Francisco Villa would shoot him as soon as he stepped on Mexican soil, and that they did not want to be responsible in that event. He asked him where he wanted to be set free, and Castillo responded that he would like to be released in Zapatista territory, an option that was discarded under the pretext that the entire country was occupied by Carrancista or Villista forces.[43]

FIG. 1. María de Jesús Flores, born in Chihuahua City, Chihuahua, the daughter of Ramón Flores and Cleofas Ugarte. She married Máximo Castillo on June 28, 1881, at the age of seventeen. According to her death certificate, she died on May 28, 1922, at the age of fifty-eight. She was buried in the community cemetery of the city of Chihuahua.

FIG. 2. Don Máximo Castillo and doña María de Jesús went to a studio to have a family photo taken with their children Atilana and Félix Castillo at the turn of the century.

FIG. 3. Photo of Castillo taken in a studio in Ciudad Juárez or El Paso during the days of the triumph over Porfirio Díaz's army in May 1911. We can assume that he had just received from the acting president, Francisco I. Madero, the appointment to the rank of colonel.

FIG. 4. Máximo Castillo on horseback, proud of his triumph, shows off a good saddle, a good saber, and a fully loaded bandolier of ammunition.

FIG. 5. Máximo Castillo, after triumphing over Porfirio Diaz's army, with one of his close friends.

FIG. 6. Máximo Castillo waits for the train close to the Hacienda de Bustillos to travel to Ciudad Juárez.

FIG. 7. Máximo Castillo riding a horse marked with the brand of Luis Terrazas.

FIG. 8. The masses greet the acting president, Francisco I. Madero, in San Pedro de las Colonias, Coahuila, in June of 1911.

FIG. 9. Photo showing some of the leaders of the Orozco movement who rose up against the government of President Francisco Madero under the banner of the Plan Orozquista in March 1912.

FIG. 10. In 1915, Máximo Castillo received a visit from his wife, son, and niece. He was transferred from Fort Bliss to Fort Wingate around the time this photo was taken.

THE SIMPLE HISTORY OF MY LIFE

MÁXIMO CASTILLO

MY FAMILY, MY VILLAGE, AND MY POVERTY

I was born on a small ranch belonging to my grandfather on May 11, 1864. The ranch belonged to the municipality of San Nicolás de Carretas.[1] I lived in the town where I first saw the light of day until 1895, when my beloved parents had died. In spite of my poverty, I did not abandon them until death took them away from me. I lived my youth without noticing life around me, working on a few small plots of land owned by my dear parents. These plots provided the livelihood of my family.

I married at the young age of seventeen, on June 28, 1881. Born September 15, 1864, my young bride was the same age as I.[2] Disgrace and misfortune befell us beginning with the day of our wedding. Twenty-two days after the wedding, I made the mistake of killing a friend of mine. As a result, I was separated from my dear young wife and put in prison for six months.

I left imprisonment in poverty, without resources of any kind, young, inexperienced, and without any knowledge of how I could earn my livelihood. I knew only a little about working in agriculture. Moreover, when I left the prison, it was not the time of the year to sow. Because of my abject poverty, I found myself obligated to leave my wife again. I went to the United States and looked for work for six long months. During my extended expedition, luck did not favor me, and I did not find work. I returned to my humble abode timid and ashamed. I was afraid to greet my wife because I did not even have five centavos to give to her after this long absence. Due to her good nature, she nonetheless received me in good spirits, as if I had brought back a million dollars.

Then I was able to rent a small plot to sow. In stark poverty and without anything to eat, I put a bit of maize and frijoles into the ground. But it did not rain that year, and nothing grew. I felt so much grief at my inability to meet my needs that I was ashamed to face my wife. I even regretted having been born, all the more so because my wife had already given birth to two children. Although my two little ones brightened up our home, my heart ached severely at seeing them naked, barefoot, and malnourished.

Our destitution grew worse despite working all of the day and part of the night. We lived a completely honorable life, without any kind of trouble or desires. My dear wife so gladly accepted our misery that she consoled me with her caresses whenever she saw me sad and beaten down. She said to me:

—Don't worry about our poverty; this is where God has put us, we are fine like this, and one day our bad luck will change.

I made an effort to improve my condition: I worked as a laborer, and I tried my hand at buying and selling merchandise. But my youth and my lack of knowledge in business matters caused my efforts to fail to produce any results.[3]

I finally decided to work a small plot of land that my father-in-law had abandoned. That plot provided the sustenance for my dear children. We lived within strict limits, but we now lived happily. In spite of our poverty, all of our neighbors appreciated us and showed us respect. And despite our most limited means, we always tried to help those who were even poorer than us within our abilities.

I never had any trouble with the authorities, but I acutely felt the unjust acts that they committed toward other poor people. Those acts made me upset, but they were impossible to remedy . . . since I did not have any influence, which was the only thing that counted. There was no justice for the poor.

In 1890, death odiously robbed me of my dear father, one of my most beloved human beings. In 1895, he redoubled his vengeance and stole my dear mother as well. After the death of my beloved parents, I no longer hesitated to abandon the unfortunate soil where I had left those who had brought me into this life. Eight days after the death of my mother, I went to the Cusihuiriáchic mine in search of work.[4] I rushed the departure from my village, after completing the rigorous state of mourning for my mother, because I had just been elected *presidente municipal* by a great majority of votes. To avoid this post, in which one could only succeed with the agreement of the *científicos*,[i] I decided to leave in a hurry.

Once at the mine, I found work. They paid me seventy-five centavos per day. After working for a few days, they paid me one peso, and shortly afterward, two pesos. I could satisfy the needs of my family with these wages, but unfortunately, this work did not last more than a year, as the mine closed down. I returned to my homeland poor as always.

Afterward, during the short time in which I worked in the "Office of Assays," I prepared a few assays for poor prospectors. I took a sample that resulted in a fabulous appraisal. The poor claimed their mine and worked there for a while. For reasons unknown to me, they [ultimately] abandoned it.

CRITICAL MISHAPS BECAUSE OF WANTING TO BE A MINER

Once their claim to the mine expired and while I was in my homeland, I claimed the mine once again. I went to Cusihuiriáchic during a very cold night in the month of January in order to be at the mine at daybreak and lay my claim to it. I was traveling on a very skinny mare. When I got to the Río Santa Cruz at midnight, I came upon a deep puddle. Unfortunately, because of the darkness of the night, I did not notice how deep it was. I lashed out at my horse, which refused to enter the puddle. I finally prevailed, but at the greatest depth of the puddle, the water rose so high that I had trouble saving my poor horse from drowning.

We left the water half-drowned . . . and completely wet . . . my good animal as well as I. I mounted [my horse], and we proceeded until we found a hill where I could make a fire and dry my clothes, which had congealed and stuck to my skin the instant we got out of the water.

I walked for a kilometer, and I accidentally found a large and dry ilex and, next to it, a few burning coals near a spot where some passersby might have taken a siesta during the day. I dismounted with difficulty, since I was stuck to my mount by ice. Half-stiff, I set the whole large

i. The educated Porfirian elite who also partnered with foreign capitalists in controlling the lion's share of Mexico's means of production.

bush on fire. I stripped completely. Stark naked, I began to dry my clothes in different places.

I soon noticed that I had made a mistake and that my shoes were already in the fire. I rushed to save them but they were beyond saving . . . they had burned. I was just thinking about my shoes when I saw the sleeves of my jacket burning. I ran to save it when I saw my shirt and underpants burning and that it was too late to save them. It was all over. I was completely naked and the cold was insufferable. My serape was the only article of clothing that had not burned. Finding myself entirely naked and aware that I would have to go to Cusihuiriáchic another day, I considered going ahead then to enter the town before dawn.

I went ahead and reached the house of a brother naked, barefoot, and half-stiff. When my brother saw me, he thought that I had lost my mind. When I told him what had happened to me, he laughed uncontrollably. He lent me some clothes.

I went to the mining agency and presented the registration of my claim to the mine, which was accepted. I started working so that I would be able to earn the money necessary to pay for the measurements. The mine was measured, and, since I had no way of working the mine, let alone pay for the title once it was issued to me, I gave half of it to an avaricious rich man in exchange for the means necessary to work and the fee for the issuance of the title.

I worked seven months like a *negro*, hoping to find a fortune at the mine. One day, we struck upon a very rich vein. There was great buzz about this discovery, and when the mining company of Cusihuiriáchic found out, the superintendent sent a representative to find out if the buzz was true. A few days later, the superintendent wrote to me letting me know that the company wanted to buy the mine from me for sixty thousand pesos, and asking if I was ready to sign a contract for the sale. That same day, I had to pay sixty-two pesos to the Fomento Ministry for the issuance of the title.

I told my business partner all of this and showed him the sample of metal that had been dug up. He sent the sample to be assayed, resulting in a certificate that valued the ore at two thousand ounces of silver per ton, and half an ounce of gold. Then he forbade me to sell to the company with which I had contracted. He did not want to pay the amount that Fomento had charged me. He took me to court in an effort to take the mine away from me. Even though there was no fair system of justice,[ii] his petition was so unjust that the authorities ruled in my favor and my partner lost all of his rights. But he stood in my way when I tried to sell when I had the opportunity to do so.

Thereafter, I continued to work miserably. [My partner] threw me overboard, and no one would offer me anything. Once I saw that the future of my children was lost because my partner had torpedoed the sale of the mine to the company that had desired to purchase it, I briefly considered killing him, but I regretted that thought later.[5] Thus I spent three years in my native land, full of misery, until the year 1901.

THE EXPEDITION TO THE NORTH IN SEARCH OF WORK

In despair after so much suffering, I went to Chihuahua City. With considerable effort, I was able to buy a small plot and build a small house so I would not have to pay rent. My family and I soon lived very happily, working to keep our sustenance.

In 1906, I had to mortgage the house for a small amount of money necessary to add a few small rooms. When the deadline to pay approached, I felt the need to embark on an expedition to the United States in search of work to save my little house that had cost me so much effort to build. Sad and downcast, I left my house on November 10, 1907.[6]

Crossing the icy, cold, and snow-covered mountains, I traversed the states of New Mexico and Texas until I reached Colorado and Wyoming.[iii] I walked day and night in the cold snow without finding anything suitable. I could not find work to earn the money that I needed. Finally, I reached a cattle ranch. There I fell ill on April 12, 1908. I could not walk any farther because of my illness, which made it impossible for me to continue on my way until May 12, 1908.

But providence desired that on the same day that I was able to go on, I found work. They paid me ten dollars and fifteen cents. By June 5,

ii. In the original, "a pesar de no haber justicia." The author refers to the weakness of the Mexican legal system, which afforded few protections to the weak and dispossessed from the depredations of wealthy land and property owners.

iii. Departing from Chihuahua City, Máximo Castillo would have reached Texas first, followed by New Mexico, Colorado, and Wyoming.

I had gathered the amount that I needed, and the following day, I left to return to my homeland, eager to arrive at my home and to see my family. Along the way, I made an observation about the coal mines and the ranches through which I passed. The poorest North Americans maintained their small houses in good order, and they had a lot of food to eat and more than enough clothes to wear. Also, along the way I saw food and clothes thrown away, and I occasionally made use of those. I asked myself: "Why is there so much misery among us Mexicans? Maybe because of our stupidity, or is our government to blame?"

The government did not take any interest in its people. Mexico has not developed any industry or agriculture, which could have given us such good results.[iv] But since the wealthy have seized most of the best lands here in Mexico, the poor cannot have a small plot of land to sow their crops. The poor are always the slaves of the large landowners. Those are the ones who take advantage of the labor of the poor: the poor man sows the soil, and the rich man reaps and enjoys the harvest. Meanwhile, the servant keeps on working for his boss without touching the fruits of his labor . . . without being able to ask for anything or assert his own rights . . . always wretched and obedient of the commands of the powerful . . . because if he said a single word in his own defense, they would send him to prison or draft him into the army.

THE FIRST CONTACT WITH THE REVOLUTION

Finally, after my long expedition, I returned to my blessed home. It was a happy moment when I saw my three loved ones: my wife and my two children.

After passing a pleasurable day with my family, I went for a walk in the streets. I encountered my friend José Sáenz. After talking for a good while, I asked him what was new, and he answered me:

—There is a lot that you don't know: an anti-reelectionist club has been formed.

—"And what is up with this club?" I asked.

iv. This perspective reflects Máximo Castillo's upbringing in rural Chihuahua. In fact, industrialization was under way in the northeastern city of Monterrey, Nuevo León, home of Latin America's largest steel foundry, and commercial agriculture had transformed much of the Mexican north.

—Its goal is to make propaganda to go to war with dictator Díaz. If you would like, go to the club so that you can find out what it is all about. I answered:

—No, I will not go to the meeting . . . I am very cowardly, and I am afraid of going to prison. I do not want to share the fate of Juan Sarabia and his comrades. There will be a denunciation; they will apprehend us while we are defenseless; and we will be off to [the infamous federal prison of] San Juan de Ulúa.[7] It is better to wait until after the elections. If there is no political resolution (and I do not think there will be), and if it is necessary to take up arms, I will be ready and then we will talk . . . See you later.

I said good-bye to my friend without worry. The next day, I met with another friend of mine, José de la Luz Fourzán. He held a book in his hand. I asked him:

—What book is that?

—It is the history of the presidents, written by don Francisco I. Madero. If you would like, take it with you so you can read it.

I answered: "With pleasure."

I read the book carefully, paying attention to all of the chapters. The book inspired me with great enthusiasm. I was frustrated because the day did not appear near when I could go and fight for my poor brothers and destroy the dictator who had held us in the cruelest servitude for so many years, since we did not even have the freedom to elect our own officeholders. I thought that we might have the liberty to elect a government that would look out for its people in the upcoming elections—a government that would give us the freedom to elect whomever we wanted so that it could govern us and make us truly free. Although I thought that such task was difficult, I wondered what would happen if we really tried . . .

I impatiently bided my time until the elections. We went to cast our votes at the voting booths, and events unfolded just as I had foreseen. After a short while, the authorities threw those of us in jail who had lined up to fill out our ballots, for the sole crime of not filling out those ballots in favor of General Díaz's candidate.

Tremulous with impatience, I wanted the revolution to start immediately in order to exact revenge for the abuses of the bad authorities. I thus lived in continuous despair, looking for the moment in which we could face off with those who oppressed the people. On occasion, I saw in my imagination those enormous fields that I had seen during the expedition to the United States during the previous year. In my mind, I could already see the poor with their small plots of land, very pretty little homes, and my fatherland in full bloom and beautiful.

Many poor neighbors lived close to my house. We were appalled to see the squalor in which they lived: they appeared ragged, almost naked, and hungry. No matter how hard they worked, there was not enough to eat. Moved by the impulse of humanity, and whenever we could, my daughter and I made sure to give them alms and our leftover food, as well as the clothes and shoes that we discarded. At times, we went too far in helping them, as we gave them our only change of clothes, but I maintained a steadfast faith that one day the situation would improve, and that we would all live in better conditions.[8]

MÁXIMO CASTILLO KEEPS HIS WORD

I thus lived through two long years until the desired day finally came. At noon on November 9, 1910, my friend José Sáenz came to my house and told me:

—My friend, the hour of bullets has already come . . . We are going to see if you will keep the promise that you made. I told Herrera. He will bring you up to date on what is happening . . . [H]e is waiting for you at his house.

—With much pleasure, I will go there right away.

At three in the afternoon, I went to Mr. Herrera's house. His wife told me that I would find him in Plaza Hidalgo. I went to the square and found him there. I greeted him and told him:

—Here I am, at your command.

—Well, comrade, Mr. José Sáenz has told me that you are willing to help us to defeat the Díaz dictatorship, which has deprived us of our liberty for so many years.

—Yes, sir; give me your orders.

—Well, do you have a room we could use?

—Yes, sir.

—Can you go to the gunpowder plant at Ocampo, bring a case of gunpowder, and take it to your house?

—Yes, sir.[9]

—Tomorrow night, we will meet at your house with several people to plan the beginning of our work, and so that you can get to know several of our comrades as well as Mr. Madero's Plan of San Luis, under which we will fight.[v]

The Plan of San Luis was read [aloud], and [the group] assigned a few tasks to its members. My commission entailed leaving post haste for Santa María de Cuevas, on the way to Santa Isabel, in order to raise [a contingent] among our supporters, and to return to Sierra Azul on November 19, near Chuviscar. We agreed to attack Chihuahua City that same day.[10]

SACRIFICING THE FAMILY

On November 11, 1910, I did not know how to inform my family about the great commitment that I had assumed. I finally decided and told my wife:

—My dear wife, I will rise up in arms to join the revolution. I am already committed, and I will need to leave on the 13th to raise the people of Santa María de Cuevas.

My wife replied:

—I will never allow you to go to war . . . How is it that you want to leave my children and me? If you are killed, what will we do by ourselves?

My wife said these words with her eyes drowned in tears. When I heard them, my chest constricted so that I could not talk for several minutes. At last, I answered her:

—See, my dear, war is now necessary, and I have to contribute my insignificant services to defeat this fiend who has kept us under his feet for so many years without giving us the freedom to speak out against his offenses.

---

v. Postdated to November 20, 1910, to avoid trouble with U.S. Neutrality Laws, the Plan of San Luis was Madero's revolutionary manifesto, which galvanized the opposition against Díaz into armed rebellion. It is considered the beginning of the Mexican Revolution.

She interrupted me:

—Let others go and offer their services; you won't go!

At that moment, my two children unexpectedly entered the room where my wife and I were having this conversation. Félix asked his mother:

—Why are you crying? What is happening between you and my daddy?

—Because your daddy says that he is going to war.

—Yes, my son; I have already made my promise, and I have to leave.

—And why do you need to go fight in the revolution? We have enough to eat and wear; let others go who need to do so. Why do you have to sacrifice yourself?

—Yes, my son, we have enough to eat, but . . . how many poor people do not even have a slice of bread? We have to sacrifice ourselves to meet the needs of those unfortunate people, our brothers.

He answered me:

—Let others go; my sister and I need you.

—See, my son, this Mr. Madero is a millionaire and does not need anything, and even so, he will sacrifice himself for the good of the poor people.

—Allow me to tell you that this is not true about this man; he will sacrifice himself for the presidency, which will give him enormous riches.

—Look, my son, he is offering to return the lands that have been taken from the poor . . . If that is so, it will be good for our people and our fatherland, and we have to help him.

—Papá, don't believe that. These men are not sacrificing themselves for the poor; instead, he will sacrifice the people for his own benefit.

—Son, I have already committed myself.

I made a few more comments, but it was impossible to convince them. Finally, my children told me:

—Do what you want, but we don't agree with you if you insist on joining the revolution . . . [W]e will stay, shedding abundant tears.

They said these words to me; but finally, when they knew that there was no other way, they realized that they could not prevent me from going to fulfill my word of honor, and that I was already committed to the cause. It was not possible to assuage my wife, but there was nothing else that I could do.[11]

THE FIRST REVOLUTIONARY TASK

On November 13, 1910, at 7:00 a.m., I took the train to Santa Isabel. Once there, I spoke to don Guadalupe Balderrama, who called himself the president of the Club Antirreeleccionista. He told me straight away that he and his son were ready, as well as ten to fifteen additional men. He showed me his weapons and some ammunition that he and his son owned.

"All right," I told him, "it is time. Be prepared by the time I return from Santa María. I have the commission of raising those people. I will come here from there straightaway, and then you and your men whom you have equipped will accompany me."

"No, sir," he answered. "I am not moving until I see don Abraham and Professor Hernández firing gunshots. Then I will go."[12]

—Don Abraham and the professor have already left Chihuahua, and I think they are already in action.

—All right, but I am not going yet.

I did not succeed in persuading him to go with me, and he would not even give me a beast of burden to continue on to Carretas even though he had two horses and a few mules in his stable. At 7:00 p.m., I was able to rent another mule from an unknown person. I stayed in Carretas overnight and then continued on to Santa Rosalía.

I talked to don Guadalupe Trevizo, a person who had promised to help the movement. He told me that it was impossible to mobilize people at that very moment because they were in the process of reaping their modest harvests. He offered to make them hurry up; he would raise them as soon as possible. He told me that he had all the people of Santa María de Cuevas on his side. I left to reach the meeting site on the agreed-upon date with my brother, Apolonio. He was the only one who accompanied me.

On the 19th, we arrived at the meeting site: the ravine of Mena. I gave an account of my commission to Mr. Cástulo Herrera, whom we recognized as our superior.[13] Mr. Herrera was in the company of twenty men, and we were waiting for Mr. Pancho Villa.

Among those of us who were there, word got around that this Mr. Villa was very valiant, and that he was a famous bandit who would bring more troops. Hearing the name of the bandit Villa produced a cold shudder in me, and I told myself: "Is it possible that I have made common cause with bandits? In the end, happen what may; I am already here."

The day went by. When night fell, an individual approached us and told Mr. Herrera that Villa would arrive at 10:00 p.m., accompanied by forty men. A little later, the shout rang out: "This time Villa is really coming!" I was astonished that I had heard his name so many times. I thought I would see a ferocious man, since I had never met a captain of bandits. Because of his reputation as a cruel murderer, he caused me horror, and I felt ashamed to find myself among those kinds of people.[14]

THE MEETING WITH PANCHO VILLA

At 9:00 or 10:00 p.m., I began to hear noises in the canyon that suggested the arrival of many people on horseback. A few minutes later, I heard more clearly: men were talking, and there was the noise of sabers. When the group came closer still, I found myself listening to a barroom conversation, but not that of undignified and drunk people. It was Villa who had angered one of his men, whom he wanted to disarm. I felt great surprise at overhearing this conversation, and great fear overpowered me, a terror so formidable that I felt my legs give way. I could not control myself.

After a few moments, he approached the fire where I sat. He greeted us courteously. We approached him, and in the light of the fire, I could see a smiling and affable face. At that point, my preconceived notions disappeared, and I realized that he was not the way I had imagined him.

[Villa] began to chat with Mr. Herrera and the other chiefs. They talked about the operations to be undertaken now that the majority of the troops had met there, as agreed, in order to attack Chihuahua City. They decided that we would march to San Andrés on November 20 to take its fortification, which was guarded by fifteen *rurales*.[vi]

We left on the afternoon of the 20th. At dawn, we laid siege to the small town. When it was daylight, we found out that the garrison had left the previous day, along with the civil authorities. We entered the

---

vi. The *rurales* were Díaz's mounted rural police force, a group noted for its corruption and brutality. Many *rurales* numbered among Mexico's most feared criminals before agreeing to turn to the side of the government.

fortification without encountering any resistance. Then they ordered Villa to go to the railroad station to see if there were troops arriving by train, as the train was due to arrive. Villa named twenty people to carry out this order, and I was one of the twenty men nominated.

We went to the station. We hid ourselves in the cuttings where firewood was stored and also concealed the weapons. The train arrived after a few minutes with three hundred Federales on board.[vii] When the train stopped, we opened fire.[15] The train immediately began to move again, and the Federales left without firing back. We later learned from the passengers that Colonel Yepes and eight soldiers had died. We did not have a single person injured; the surprise attack went so well that they did not have time to fire back, and we did not let them lean out of the windows [to shoot at us].

We stayed in San Andrés for two days. I did not notice there the supposed disorder and banditry caused by Villa and his men. However, when we went to Santa Isabel, I witnessed precisely the chaos that he and his men created. They sacked all of the stores, and his men left these stores with jars of butter and whatever other merchandise they had found. I felt such repugnance at seeing the disorder associated with banditry that I almost got to the point of leaving the group and no longer serving the revolution. But the need to stay true to my word made me go on.

We left for Chihuahua City on November 26 and slept in a ranch named Los Toriles located two leagues from the city. The morning of the 27th, Mr. Herrera ordered Villa and ten of his men to embark for Nombre de Dios in order to see if they could find our people waiting for us to attack the city; and he also sent Mr. Santos Estrada and Guadalupe Gardea along with fifteen other people from Parral.[viii]

At a place called El Tecolote, when we marched along the wagon road, we encountered the rearguard of the troops of General Juan Navarro, who had been sent in our pursuit. They took the fight to us right away. When we heard loud explosions, Mr. Herrera, don Seferino Pérez,

vii. Federales was the name by which most Mexicans referred to soldiers in the Federal army.

viii. The meaning of this sentence is not clear because Castillo omits the destination of this second group.

and I ran toward the source of these detonations. When we drew near the location of the fighting, we saw that the vanguard consisting of eight hundred men had turned around near the hacienda of Fresno in order to render assistance.

Mr. Herrera ordered don Seferino to run and tell the people to retreat immediately because there were too many enemies. Don Seferino ran, and when he arrived at our positions, his horse was killed. Our people retreated, leaving seven comrades dead and seven more prisoners. Mr. Santos Estrada was among the dead. The enemy attempted to besiege all of us, and we ran away. The comrades escaped, some on foot and others on horseback in pairs and without sombreros.

We retreated to the ravine of Mena, the site of our encampment on November 19 and 20. That night, all of the troops gathered, and the next day, we went to the district of Guerrero to join the forces of Pascual Orozco, who had already taken the city of Guerrero as we had heard.

A PROBLEM OF LEADERSHIP: OROZCO OR CÁSTULO HERRERA?

On December 4, 1910, we encountered Orozco and his troops in La Junta. There were several disagreements among the chiefs. It seemed that Herrera wanted to be the supreme chief of the revolution, and Orozco did as well.[16] There was a moment of great disappointment after a telegrapher among the revolutionaries told Mr. Herrera that he had sent telegrams to Sonora, Sinaloa, and other states asking what the local residents said about the revolution, only to find out that nothing was said in those areas, and that the rumor was that the revolution was active [only] in Chihuahua. For that reason, they believed that we were the only revolutionaries in the entire republic.

Finally, Orozco marched with his troops to Cerro Prieto, a place known to be held by the federal government. Mr. José de la Luz Blanco marched to Temósachic, and Mr. Herrera, to Chihuahua City. Villa went to the hacienda del Rosario, where he took three thousand pesos from the administrator as well as a fine horse.

In mid-December, after five days of marching, we, the followers of Mr. Herrera, found ourselves at the hacienda of Torreón, seven leagues from Chihuahua City. There, a man reached us to let us know that Villa was under siege in San Andrés, and that we needed to go help him out.

We returned soon thereafter. A few days later, we were already in the outskirts of San Andrés when we found out that Villa had left the village without further ado. At that moment, a letter from Orozco to Dolores Palomino and Guadalupe Gardea arrived, which instructed them to gather all valiant men who would like to accompany him. The letter also ordered them to disarm Mr. Cástulo Herrera and to take the money that he had on his person. [Palomino and Gardea] showed [Herrera] the order that they had received from Orozco. They invited him to join [Orozco's forces]. Herrera replied that he would not be able to join Orozco because he did not get along well with him, and that he would go to El Paso, Texas, to see if he was right about don Abraham González. If he found [González] there and received any ammunition from him, [Herrera] agreed to send it to them. He showed them the money he carried: five hundred pesos. He gave Palomino two hundred pesos and left three hundred.

Soon thereafter, [Herrera] invited me to accompany him on his way to the border. I told Palomino and Gardea that I was going to go with Mr. Herrera, and that it would have been very difficult for me to refuse his request since I had risen up in arms on his side. I told them that if [Herrera] went with the intention of staying [in El Paso], I was going to return and join them. I would bring them any ammunition that he would be able to procure. We split from the group accompanied by six additional men.[17]

We went to El Paso and met with don Abraham. Mr. Herrera informed don Abraham of the miserable state of the revolutionaries, the scarcity of weapons and ammunition, and the disagreements among the chiefs of the group.[18]

—"There are 16,000 cartridges," said don Abraham. "Who will take them with him?"

—"Here is Mr. Castillo," said Herrera.

I answered: "Yes, sir, I will take them to my comrades."

They gave me the ammunition in the railroad station Valentein [*sic*], on the line running from El Paso to Laredo, Texas. I moved the ammunition to Barrancas de Guadalupe on the Mexican side of the border. Six men joined me in El Paso in order to accompany me. They carried a letter to a Mr. Jesús Sáenz, who lived on the Mexican side. The letter contained instructions to order the troops under his command to accompany him in his mission. Sáenz's group included a number of men who were partisans of the revolution. Although they were not fighters and acted as noncombatants, they were armed. Ten of these men joined the six men who were already with me, all on foot. Then I went to the small village of Las Barrancas and took fourteen skinny horses and bad saddles before retiring to the sierra.

Four days later, I arrived at the hacienda of Calderón. Upon our arrival, all of our horses were tired. I took twenty healthy horses and continued on my way, traveling night and day. I reached General Orozco in the hacienda of San Isidro on January 28, 1911. The troops of La Mojina were just returning from the battle that had taken place the day before. When the general noticed that I was bringing the ammunition, he came out to greet me and ordered the trumpets to sound reveille. He greeted me affectionately and told me:

—You are the only man who carries out his mission. We have already sent several people to bring ammunition, and they have not returned since.

ALL TOWARD CD. JUÁREZ: THE FIRST ATTEMPT

I gave [Orozco] the messages that don Abraham had sent him, and I verbally let him know that don Abraham wanted all revolutionary groups to advance toward Cd. Juárez to take over its fortress, which had only a paltry garrison.[19]

We left for Juárez that same night. We arrived at Moctezuma station and stopped four trains, two passenger and two freight trains. We boarded one of the engines and destroyed a great part of the tracks. We boarded our horses and continued to Juárez aboard the passenger trains without bothering anyone. On February 1, at 4:00 p.m., we arrived at the station of Samalayuca.

Then he gave the orders that the passenger trains should continue on to Juárez,[ix] and that a group of sixty men should ride a train engine toward Juárez and destroy all the bridges, getting as close to that city as possible. At 8:00 p.m., the group left with ten cases of gunpowder. At 11:00 p.m., we heard a great thunderclap in our encampment. We

ix. It is not clear from the context who gave this order. Most likely, it was Abraham González.

all shouted with glee: "Long live the Revolution! Our comrades have already blown up the first bridge!" We waited for them to return, but they did not come back all night.

At daybreak, one of the comrades returned and rendered an account to General Orozco. The enemy had surprised them in the station of Mesa where they had removed one of the tracks, which caused the engine of the train to derail. They had opened fire, and the explosion that we had heard was the gunpowder that had blown up in the gunfire. The comrade believed that the enemy held our men under siege. Right away, the general ordered Mr. Mariano Hernández and his thirty men to render assistance to our comrades, while the rest of us unloaded the horses from the train so that we could send more reinforcements.

The first horses to be unloaded from the train were my own. Without waiting for instructions, I ordered ten comrades near me to saddle up right away and go to the assistance of our comrades. I was in a great hurry because four of my men were there, and I wanted to know what had happened to them. I arrived at the site of the disaster, and there was Mr. Hernández, who asked me:

—When will the other people be here?

—No, sir, I don't think anyone else will come.

—They are still disembarking very slowly; it's a bad deal. Orozco offered me to send people as reinforcements, even though there is no enemy here. But if the enemy were indeed here and you had not come, they would have sacrificed me. I will tell you that the danger has not passed. There are very few of us, and we are close to Juárez, less than three miles. They can easily figure out how many of us are here and return to annihilate us. Orozco should come later.

I told him:

—Let's go and bury our comrades.

Two of my four comrades had been killed, and the other two were missing. We buried the dead, and since no enemy was in sight, I asked Mr. Hernández to stay there with me, just in case Orozco arrived with all of his men, even if by night.

We slept there. By morning, Orozco had not come. He arrived around 1:00 p.m. and gave the order to advance upon Bauche, a station of the Ferrocarril del Noroeste. He believed that it was possible that don José de la Luz Blanco would arrive in the train from Nuevo Casas Grandes, since he had offered his assistance.

We got to the station of Bauche at 3:00 p.m. that same day, February 3, 1911. Right away, Orozco gave the order to remove one of the tracks in order to stop the train in case the enemy came, and that we should take up appropriate positions. We did so. The train was scheduled to come in at 5:00 p.m. The hour passed, and the train did not arrive. At 6:00 p.m., Orozco received a letter from don Abraham instructing him "to go get some ammunition on the Mexican side of the border close to La Esmelta."[20] Then he ordered me to go, because, as he put it, I was the most qualified man for these tasks.

Soon thereafter, I left with ten men to get the ammunition. At 9:00 p.m. that night, the train arrived, carrying a Porfirian general by the name of Rábago in place of Blanco. I retrieved the ammunition and waited for Orozco in the ranch of Flores, where I handed it over to him. On February 7, we approached the [Rio Grande] on the other side of La Esmelta, and the following day, a column of Federales came to encounter us. We had a small skirmish and repelled them.

THE ARRIVAL OF FRANCISCO I. MADERO'S GENERAL STAFF

We stayed there for three days. Orozco continued to communicate with don Abraham, and on the morning of February 9, 1911, he sent a man to tell us to saddle up and retreat. I saddled up my horse and asked the general where we were going. He said:

—We will take Ascensión and Casas Grandes. Both are fortresses of minor importance, because I don't think that we can take Juárez. We don't have enough people.

Orozco left with his men, and I was ready to leave when Mr. Manuel Aldana came and told me:

—Mr. Castillo, yesterday at 11:00 p.m., ten to twelve gentlemen arrived at Orozco's encampment. They said that they belonged to Mr. Madero's General Staff and will join us. But Orozco ignored them; he has already departed and left them there. They are all in a huff,[x] and they say that one of Mr. Madero's brothers is on his way.[21]

---

x. In the original, "están hechos montón."

I mounted my horse and galloped to their position. They were already going up a hill. Right away, I said:

—Gentlemen, excuse me, please tell me who you are and what you are doing.

One of the gentlemen responded in a loud voice:

—We are your supporters; we came last night to spend time with the general, but he did not want us in his company. He departed and left us there. We don't have any weapons, and we were going to climb this hill to find shelter until the night when we can pass over to the other side, because once the Federales find out that you left, they can come and kill us.

—Gentlemen, they tell me that a brother of Sr. Madero is among you.

—"Yes, sir," a young man of approximately twenty years of age replied. "I am Raúl Madero, at your service."

Then the one with the loud voice:

—I am Eduardo Hay.

—And I am Roque González.

Thus all of the men gave me their names in succession.

—Gentlemen, although I do not know you, it is enough for me to know that this young man is a brother of Mr. Madero; I am here at your service, and please let me know what you need me to do.

—We would like you to protect us.

—Then please give me your orders.

I then sent a man to catch up with Mr. Mariano Hernández, who had already started to walk. He returned, and I told him:

—Mr. Hernández, here are these men who will join us; they are from Mr. Madero's General Staff, and this young man is a brother of Mr. Madero. They came last night, and Orozco did not want us there. He departed and left us here by ourselves. If you would like, accompany me so that we can protect them.

—"With pleasure, Mr. Castillo," Mr. Hernández replied.

With much indignation, the old man took off his sombrero, and before greeting the gentlemen, he said:

—Gentlemen, please excuse my bad vocabulary, but I have never seen a procession as . . . as Orozco's in my entire life.

Then he greeted them and told them:

—Here you have at your command my comrade Castillo and myself. Then I asked my men to get a little bit of flour that we had with us and to make a few tortillas. The men in the group had told me that they were very hungry, but we hardly had enough flour to make one tortilla for each of them. Afterward, I told them:

—If you would like, we will go to the Flores ranch right over there. We can at least find water there, and let's see what we can eat. There are a few lean goats.

Then Mr. Hay sent a man with a piece of paper to give a report to Mr. Madero and don Abraham of the events regarding Orozco, giving high praise to Mr. Hernández and me. We went to the ranch and stayed there for two days eating the unsalted meat of lean goats.

CASTILLO, CHIEF OF THE ESCORT OF FRANCISCO I. MADERO

On February 11, 1911, Mr. Hay told us to go to the village of Zaragoza to protect the passage of Mr. Madero and don Abraham. We marched with our column consisting of eighty-six men. That night, I received orders to bring a wagon with ammunition and provisions located on the riverbank. On the night of the 12th, Mr. Madero and don Abraham passed through. Then Mr. Roque González Garza introduced me to Mr. Madero and told him of my good conduct toward his men. I told him that they would have probably found themselves in danger if I had not protected them at the site where Orozco had left them. Then Mr. Madero said:

—I need an escort, and you will be its chief . . . I want you to be by my side at all times.

—With much pleasure, sir; I will do everything possible to fulfill my duty.

From that moment on, my men and I had twice as much work as before, standing guard day and night in the headquarters of Mr. Madero. On the 13th· we departed Zaragoza in the direction of San Agustín, and on the 14th, we went to Guadalupe. There was a group of PLM supporters there under the command of Mr. Prisciliano Silva, and since they did not want to support Mr. Madero, we disarmed them and their men.[22]

On the 16th, we left for Villa Ahumada and then proceeded to Alamos de Peña, Carmen, and San Lorenzo. On March 1, we arrived at San

Buenaventura, where a large number of revolutionary comrades awaited us who were under the command of Mr. Flores Alatorre and other chiefs. We agreed to attack a federal contingent that defended Casas Grandes.

On the 4th, we went to Galeana, and on the 5th, we proceeded to the ranch of Anchoncho, only two kilometers from the town of Casas Grandes. That same night we went to reconnoiter the place from where we intended to attack the town. We approached a few hills only one kilometer from the fortress. We also reconnoitered the positions of the enemy. We could see the soldiers preparing their fortifications at the western side of the town. In a large house, we saw a headquarters, and two soldiers who were carrying bags of sand up to the parapets.

—"What's over there?" asked Mr. Madero.

—It is the headquarters of the enemy, and they are getting ready for combat.

—Send eight to ten men to throw them out of that place.

—No, sir, it is not that easy. There are a lot of them.

—Yes, fellow, you can throw them out; they are very cowardly.

—Well, but let's wait until dawn so that our entire force can enter the village; why would we fight them right now?

—All right, leave a few people there who can watch these positions so that they don't reinforce them tonight. We will have to be there to-morrow.

—Very well, sir.

DEFEAT IN CASAS GRANDES

I left twenty men to guard the positions, and we retired to the camp. During the night, we planned the attack. On March 6, 1911, at 4:00 a.m., we went ahead, and at 5 a.m., we opened fire. Mr. Madero, the men who formed our escort, and I arrived at the position of the *montezumas.* We heard loud shooting on all sides. Once I had stationed my people in the *montezumas,* we opened fire on the church and other points where one could see the enemy far away, and I began to see that our enemies hit their targets. I wondered why the enemy was able to aim so well from such a great distance until they shot a bullet through a skylight that hit its target in the forehead of one of my comrades. I realized that there were enemy troops in a few small houses that were no more than fifty meters away from our positions.[23]

Meanwhile, Madero sat by a stream at the rear of our positions, together with General José de la Luz Soto, who, it seemed, had arrived proclaiming that [the Federales] had cut him off from the rest of the column and that they had not allowed him to enter the town. He said that they had laid an ambush at the point where he was going to enter. When Madero heard that the enemy had killed one of our comrades, he came to see the dead man. The enemy showered us with gunshots, and several of the bullets barely missed Mr. Madero's head. He asked me:

—What is this buzzing noise?

—It comes from the bullets that scream like that. Sir, get away from here and go back to your place because they will kill you here.

—No, my dear fellow, they are very bad at shooting.

—No, sir, you have the proof right here.

He retired; and a few moments later we heard a reveille. I asked General Soto:

—What does this reveille mean?

—I could not hear it very well, but it seemed like "ranch" and "dispatch." Maybe they are conceding a position.

In fact, however, the reveille announced the fact that reinforcements were arriving. A bit later, around 8:00 a.m., we began to observe that our people were scattering in different directions, and then I observed a number of comrades running away on the right flank, followed by cavalry. We could also see a nearby cannon opening fire on our positions. I saw that more comrades were retreating on the left flank, firing at the enemy and pursued by more cavalry. At that point, I noticed that the majority of my men had gone, and that I had no more than ten men left. General Soto had already mounted a cart that stood there along with a bunch of mules. I then told Mr. Madero:

—Let's go; all of our people have run away, and they have us under siege.

He replied indignantly:

—Why are we leaving?

—Sir, because there is no other way; all of our people have fled; the enemy is here in large numbers, and there are only a few of us remaining here.

He answered:

—Why are we running?

—Sir, do not think that what I am saying is due to cowardice. Go away and give me your orders, I will stay here, but I don't consider it a sign of either wisdom or intelligence for a great man who stands for a cause [to remain in the line of fire]. Similarly, it is no good if they kill us, but if they kill you, it will be the end of the revolution.

He finally understood me and began to walk very slowly. A soldier and I took him in our middle. I ordered my men to follow us. We had not even walked five steps when a bullet struck my comrade who was walking on Mr. Madero's right side. The bullet hit him in the back and killed him instantly. Mr. Madero stretched out his hand to take the dead man's carbine, and at once, another bullet struck him in the arm.

—"They have already wounded you," I told him, because I saw him drop the carbine.

—I don't think so; they hit the carbine. It bounced, and my arm fell asleep.

We kept walking and stopped when we reached a stream about ten steps ahead. I lifted up the sleeve of his tight-fitting shirt, because I saw that he was moving his fingers a lot as if to find out whether he was injured. Then I saw the little stream of blood and the bullet hole.[24]

—"Yes, they wounded me," Madero said.

We continued onward. Once we arrived at a small and open plain, I saw a group of cavalry very near on our left who were cutting off our retreat. In our rear, an infantry unit armed with a cannon pursued us, raining bullets from a distance of two hundred meters. On the right was more cavalry. The rain of bullets and cannonballs was so rich, not to mention the large number of grenades that fell in our midst, that we had no choice but to drop down to the ground.

—"Let yourself fall, Mr. Madero," I advised him.

And he answered:

—"Why? One gets knocked down a lot."

I was sorry to hear his answer, and when a grenade exploded, I found myself obligated to remain standing. I looked at the countenance of all of us. I could see the terror in the eyes of my comrades. Flushed to the earlobes, Mr. Madero's face betrayed irritation. I said to myself: "either this gentleman does not know that bullets kill, or he is very brave."

When I realized that the cavalry on our left had already passed us and appeared poised to impede our way out, I talked to Captain Francisco Alvarado, who was firing at the enemy on my right along with six men. I told him:

—Switch to the left and protect us from this cavalry.

They ran to the left, and because the enemy was close, they were able to kill two of their soldiers. When the Federales saw two of their comrades fall, they stopped for a moment and let us pass.[25]

Once we got to the ranch of Anchoncho where our encampment was located, we found a young man riding a horse and another horse at his side. I ran and took the horses from the youngster and told Mr. Madero:

—Ride one of these horses.

—No, fellow, they are very skinny.

Soon thereafter, I saw another gentlemen farther in the distance, riding another horse with yet another mount already saddled up. I approached the man and told him:

—Lend us this horse so that Mr. Madero can ride it.

—Yes, sir; that's why I brought it.

That man was Mr. Hinojosa, who had been sent to find us. Then Mr. Madero mounted his horse and rode to the encampment. I followed him, occasionally firing at the enemy. We arrived at the camp with very few men, and meanwhile, the majority of the other troops were climbing up the hills. There was Mr. Madero, very angry, pleading with General Soto to stop the men and offer the enemy more resistance. Soto told him that it was impossible, and that the men who had fled were demoralized. At last, we convinced [Madero] that we should follow these people because the enemy was almost on top of us.

We went to the hacienda of San Diego.

After Mr. Madero told don Abraham and his entire General Staff about the tight situation in which we had found ourselves before our flight, as well as about my insistence that he leave the battle scene, he thanked me and gave his apologies. He told me that he would not be so stubborn next time around, and that he would not place me in such a difficult position again. Garibaldi, Raúl, and all of his General Staff made great amends to me, and Mr. Madero ordered a local photographer to take a picture of him and me. The picture featured me at his back, indicating that I was his guard. He sent this photograph to his parents; when I met them later on at the encampment at Esmeralda, they told me that they already knew me. They had already seen me in a photograph that their son had sent them and knew that I took good care of him.

THE REVOLUTION TRIUMPHS IN CIUDAD JUÁREZ

We stayed at this hacienda for several days and brought the people back together who had dispersed. We left for Galeana on March 11, 1911, to join Orozco, whose ranks already included approximately two thousand men. On the 13th, we marched to the hacienda of Bustillos together with Orozco.[26] On the 17th, we camped on the bank of the lagoon of Encinillas, on the western side facing the [train] station. There were several Federales at the train station. Once they saw our camp, they fired at us with their machine guns, at a distance of four kilometers, rather than going out and attacking us. Because the bullets did not even reach the midway point of the lagoon, we weren't worried. We continued to unsaddle our horses and procured food by killing a few little lambs from a herd that we were taking to Bustillos.

The enemy withdrew in the evening, and they did not believe that we would attack. We continued our march. On the 24th, we reached Bustillos and stayed there for a few days, reorganizing the groups of revolutionaries that had dispersed all over the place in disorderly fashion.

On April 1, Mr. Madero went to visit the city of Guerrero. He was deeply moved when he pronounced his discourse, and he cried when he greeted a group of mourning widows whose husbands had died in Cerro Prieto at the beginning of the revolution. We returned to Bustillos, and on the 10th, we marched northeast toward Juárez until we reached Las Varas, the terminus of the railroad track. There, Salazar and Mr. Madero had their first disagreement, because Salazar told [Madero] that he was not an anti-reelectionist but, instead, a member of the Partido Liberal Mexicano.

On the 13th we continued the march to kilometer 84, the location of the other railroad terminus. On the 14th, we embarked for Guzmán again. On the 16th, the vanguard proceeded toward Juárez, and on the 17th, our army had its first encounter with the enemy's vanguard in the station of Bauche. On the 18th, Mr. Madero ordered Salazar and all the Liberal chiefs who accompanied him to lay down their weapons. Once they were disarmed and arrested, I received the order to watch over them and transfer them to Ciudad Guerrero. That same night, a train with more of our troops departed in the direction of Juárez. On the 19th, we went to the rearguard with Mr. Madero, and the prisoners were sent to Guerrero.[27]

From Bauche, we proceeded by land to the ranch of Flores. On the 21st, we went to the river and made camp on the riverbank and the border facing La Esmelta.

We stayed there for a few days while Mr. Madero conducted negotiations with the delegates of Porfirio Díaz. After these negotiations ended fruitlessly, on May 7, Mr. Madero ordered us to retreat. In his view, we should not attack Cd. Juárez because doing so might provoke the intervention of the United States. Orozco, Villa, the other officers, and I did not agree, and we all protested against the retreat, but Mr. Madero insisted on our withdrawal. Madero moved his own camp, but none of the other camps made preparations to leave.

Orozco and Villa went into hiding, and at dusk, Villa told me to send Mr. Madero to him, guarded by a few men. He told me to pick ten of my best men to help with this endeavor. By dawn of the next day, they were going to attack Cd. Juárez, and Villa and Orozco were not going to withdraw without attacking. I signaled my understanding. Mr. Madero and I continued to look for Orozco and Villa so that they would move their encampments, but it was no use: we searched but they remained in hiding.

At 8:00 p.m., Madero received a telegram authored by several revolutionary chiefs, which announced that Porfirio Díaz had just tendered his resignation. For that reason, we did not move from our site. At 7:00 a.m. on Dec. 8, we received a telegram refuting Díaz's resignation.[28]

At 11:00 a.m. that same day, when the people saw the opposition of Mr. Madero, four rebel soldiers opened fire against the Federales; soon thereafter, others followed suit. When Mr. Madero found out that our men were on the attack, he became very angry and ordered a cease-fire. Those who did not obey would be shot. He sent a man with a white flag to the entrance of Juárez with the charge of entering the city and telling Navarro that the rebels were suspending the attack, and that

Madero was going to withdraw his men. But it was not possible for the flag bearer to enter Juárez, as he faced gunfire from both the enemy and our comrades. Mr. Madero personally worked hard to detain the people [eager for an attack,] but it was already impossible; large groups of revolutionaries were coming from different directions.

At 3:00 p.m., seeing that it was impossible to contain the troops any longer, Madero gave the orders to continue the attack, to put the cannons in position, and to tell Orozco and Villa to provide good leadership for the attack. The battle lasted day and night until May 10, 1911, when the garrison surrendered at 2:00 p.m.

Both sides had suffered approximately two hundred casualties. They took six hundred prisoners as well as several mountain cannons and machine guns. General Navarro and his General Staff were detained in a room where Mr. Madero lived; and I received the order to watch over them. I was told that my supervision of the prisoners had the primary objective of preventing abuses on the part of some of our comrades; we were to treat them with respect and honor.[29]

OROZCO AND VILLA REBEL AGAINST FRANCISCO I. MADERO

The days went by. One day, at approximately 10:00 a.m., I arrived at the headquarters escorting Mr. Madero with ten men. I already had ten more men stationed there to relieve those who had gone with me. When we arrived, I noticed that there were several armed soldiers in formation, and still more soldiers were coming from Villa's and Orozco's quarters. I thought that there would be a meeting of some kind.

Mr. Madero entered the headquarters, which served as a makeshift presidential palace, where his men were already waiting for him. I was just giving orders to the guard when Villa spoke to me:

—Comrade, line up here with my men; I need you.

—"Very well," I replied.

And he walked away. After he entered the headquarters, I approached an officer who had his troops lined up in formation.

—"What is this about?" I asked.

—I don't know, sir. They gave us orders to line up here; I don't know what for.

And he added:

—Armed soldiers are emerging in formation from all quarters. Right away, I attempted to enter the headquarters to find out what these movements were about. At that moment, I observed that Villa was dragging Mr. Madero out of the headquarters, and that Mr. Madero was resisting. I ran toward him, parting the crowd to where Villa was attempting to drag Mr. Madero out the door. I heard Villa tell him:

—Walk! Walk!

And Mr. Madero answered:

—Why are you taking me away?

Meanwhile, my brother, Apolonio, and Carlos Aguirre stood guard by the door. One of them grabbed Mr. Madero and the other, Villa, and separated them. Once he saw himself freed from Villa's claws, Madero shouted:

—Shoot Villa!

Villa ran to his quarters to summon more troops, and Mr. Madero walked toward a parked automobile. I noticed that Orozco was following him, saying:

—Go ahead and surrender.

Right away, I embraced [Madero] with my left arm, with my pistol in my other hand pointing at Orozco, who was also following us with a pistol in his hand.

Mr. Madero got into the automobile; he sat down on the top,[xi] and Orozco got into the driver's seat. I stayed on the footrest without taking my eyes off Orozco's movements, and I ordered my twenty men to get ready to shoot, depending on Orozco's next move.

At that moment, Raúl Madero arrived.

—"Castillo," he said, "I don't have a weapon."

—"Take my pistol," I said.

He took my pistol, stood on the footrest of the automobile, and fixed his gaze upon Orozco. I took my rifle; all of us were looking at Orozco. As soon as he got into the car, Mr. Madero began to shout at the troops who were present.

—Whom do you obey: Orozco or me?

Some shouted "you"; others, "Orozco"; and yet others, "both of you!"

xi. In the original, "se paró arriba."

Orozco and Mr. Madero were trying to figure out who had the upper hand. Orozco told him:

—Give yourself up as a prisoner, Madero.

—"Do not use your pistol," Mr. Madero told him.

—"If it is necessary, I will use it," Orozco replied

—"Fellow," answered Mr. Madero, "give me a hug! Everything is settled."

—No, sir, give yourself up as a prisoner. You are a useless man, totally useless; you are not capable of providing food to the people . . . How will you be able to be president? You are an arrogant man; you lie when you say that your brothers have spent their capital in service of the revolution . . . [T]hey have not even spent a single centavo."

These were only some of the insults that Orozco hurled; and then Mr. Madero shouted to the troops:

—Everything is settled; you will now all have enough to eat and dress.

And he insisted on Orozco shaking hands with him; at last, Orozco obliged, following the pleas and entreaties of many people who urged him to shake hands with Madero.

After the handshake, Orozco got out of the automobile, his eyes streaked with tears. Mr. Madero boarded another automobile and rapidly drove to the site where the [Porfirian] prisoners were held. He talked to General Navarro, made him get into the automobile, and took him to the bank of the river. Then Navarro passed over to the other side, but not before telling Madero:

—I am your prisoner of war; if you need me tomorrow so that I can be shot, I will be ready at the time that you desire.

Mr. Madero returned to the headquarters and had another argument with Villa, but they soon came to an agreement. The troops had returned to their quarters.[30]

On the afternoon of that same day, Mr. Madero gathered his siblings and friends, his father, his mother, his attorneys and engineers at his house. All of them commented on the events that had just occurred, and especially on the grave danger in which Mr. Madero had found himself. Manuel Urquidi, an engineer, told Mr. Madero's parents about the way I had behaved during those critical moments. He told them:

—I saw it all. Mr. Castillo was in the middle of the street when Villa was dragging Mr. Madero to the door. Once he saw how Villa was treating Madero, he ran, dividing the crowd by throwing people to one side or the other, like a *golón* horse, until he reached the spot where Madero was. He put his arm around him, and they went to the automobile. He had one arm around him; he carried a pistol with his other hand with which he warded off Orozco.[31]

After hearing these observations, [Madero's] father and mother approached me and gave me their effusive thanks and appreciation. With tears in her eyes, the lady put me in charge of her son, telling me not to leave him alone even for one moment. One day, she said, I would receive recompense for my good behavior. I told them that I had not done any more than fulfill my duty, and that I would do everything possible to continue to do so as far as my strength would carry me.

MÁXIMO CASTILLO ACCOMPANIES MADERO TO MEXICO CITY

At last, don Porfirio resigned, and don Francisco installed [Francisco] León de la Barra as provisional president. Then Mr. Madero left for the capital via North American territory.

I received the list of those who were going to accompany Mr. Madero to Mexico City, and Lieutenant Terrazas and I were on this list. Then Mr. Madero spoke to me and said:

—You and Terrazas are on the list of those who will travel with me. Leave your troops at the orders of don Abraham.

—"Very well," I answered.

After we had departed for Mexico City, Roque González Garza told me during a conversation along the way:

—Actually, you were not going to accompany us, but Garibaldi and I convinced Mr. Madero. He had given the orders for you not to come along.

This news surprised me, but I answered coldly that I would not have come if I had known beforehand. Rather than traveling to Mexico City, I had greater desire to go to Chihuahua City, where my family resided. So we continued on until we arrived in Mexico City; and four or five days later, we visited the states of Morelos and Guerrero.

The objective of Mr. Madero's visit was to see the forces of General

[Emiliano] Zapata and to order the disarmament of the revolutionary armies. We went to Chilpancingo, the capital of the state of Guerrero, and then returned to Mexico City. Terrazas and I stayed on as guards, stationed at the entrance of the house where Madero lived. On the morning of June 20, 1911, he told us in simple terms:

—Well, guys, go home; I don't need you here anymore. Go and see the people you left behind. Form a corps of *rurales* and teach them discipline; teach them how to march. Once I am president, we'll see if you come back here. Talk to Eduardo Hay; he should give you three hundred pesos and your safe conducts.

We went to see Hay. On the way, I told my comrade, Terrazas:

—Wow. How ungentlemanly is this man, and how little gratitude does he have? Everyone else would have told us the same: "I don't need you anymore." But at least he would have said: "Thank you very much. I am appreciative of your good or bad services."

We soon found Mr. Hay; he told us:

"I have orders to give you three hundred pesos and your safe conducts, but you should know, Mr. Castillo, that I appreciate you."

—Thank you, sir!

—Don't think that there is nothing else to do in the revolution; I am also your friend, and I wish you could always be here with us. What work do you want here?

—Sir, I don't know my way around here, and even less, how to find work, but I will tell you in all honesty that I do not want work . . . I am not fighting to do work of any kind . . . The revolution is already over, and I will work as always—working in order to live.

—"Well, you already know that I am at your service if I can help you in any way," said Mr. Hay.

—Well, taking advantage of your good manners, I would appreciate it if you could use your influence to help me recoup the minor expenses that I incurred as a result of participating in the revolution . . . They say that they will be reimbursed . . . I was so stupid that I sacrificed what little I had to buy weapons and ammunition, and it is possible that I could lose my little house, because I mortgaged it and the deadline for payment is coming up.

—You will be paid with priority and as a first preference.

He gave us the three hundred pesos, and we went to Gobernación Palace so that we could receive the order for the safe conducts. *Licenciado* Emilio Vásquez Gómez, the secretary of gobernación, asked us if we were already leaving.

—"Yes, sir," we answered.

—Well, I don't agree with you leaving, because you have been the people who protected Madero during the most critical moments, and he is still in danger.

—Sir, he has already given us our leave and told us that he no longer needs us.

—Yes, he does need you. Go and tell him on my behalf that I don't agree with letting you go. I will go to talk to him in the evening to the effect that he should let you continue to serve as his guard.

—Very well, sir.

We went and shared with Mr. Madero the opinion of the secretary of gobernación. He replied:

—Well, if don Emilio doesn't want you to go then . . . But I don't need you anymore. I am not in danger, because everyone loves me very much. I am going to Tijuana; and I am going to stay there until the elections . . . [T]here, I have six or eight hundred men.

Upon hearing this, his wife said:

—I don't agree that these guys should leave, either. Although you say that everyone loves you and that you have eight hundred men . . . You will have thousands, but not people you can trust like these two, who sacrificed themselves for you at the time of greatest danger.

—No, my dear; let them go; they will love to see their families.

So we said good-bye; and then we went to bid farewell to his parents and other siblings as well. Don Gustavo asked us:

—Why are you leaving?

—Mr. Madero has relieved us from our charge because he does not need us anymore.

—What do you mean he doesn't need you anymore? Once you have left, they will stab him to death.

—Maybe not; he said that he is well loved.

—That they will love him . . . he is crazy. But if there is no other way, and if he already told you that you needed to leave, then go.

We then went to don Pancho's house and did not find him. But we tried to say good-bye to the lady [the mother of Francisco I. Madero], and she also asked us why we were leaving. When we told her the reason, she answered:

—He is not in charge. I am in charge, and you are not going until I tell you to. We will see Pancho.

I refused to go and told the lady:

—You go, along with Mr. Terrazas.

They got into a car and drove to Tacubaya. There, the lady spoke with her son.

—Why are you letting these fellows go? You need them to guard you.

After a long discussion, Terrazas told me:

—Mr. Madero finally agreed that we should not leave, but it was probably in order not to upset his mother.

We spent ten days dealing with these difficulties. We spent the 150 pesos that he had given us, as our needs required us to do so.

But on July 1, [Madero] ordered us to leave in definitive fashion. And since we had already spent all of our money, we had to spend the time of our trip to Chihuahua without any food with the exception of fifty centavos worth of bananas that we bought on the train. Friends with whom Terrazas shared the story of how we had been treated told us that they could not believe that [Madero] had sent his chiefs of escort home in such condition. In fact, though, it had happened that way.

CASTILLO RESPECTS THE DECISION OF THE PEOPLE (AND MAKES IT COUNT)

Once we had returned to Chihuahua, I made an appointment with the governor, don Abraham, and I showed him the order I had received to form a corps of *rurales* with the people who had accompanied me in the revolution. He told me.

—Try, then, to discharge as many people as you can find, at least 150 and up to 300, so that they can form your corps of *rurales* and return to the villages where they grew up. In Carretas, I will try to come to an agreement with the leadership of all the villages, because I receive complaints each day that the people don't agree with their local authorities. They also resent the banditry that has developed there on a large scale.

Among my troops in the revolution, the majority were railroad workers who earned three or four pesos; they were waiting for me to dismiss them. I asked don Abraham how much they were going to be paid, and he told me one peso and forty centavos. From that amount, they would have to pay the grazing fee for their horses. I pointed out to him how much they were going to earn. My men asked for their discharge and retired from active duty.[32] I also desired to retire to private life, but my own critical circumstances and the wish to help my people in some way convinced me to serve the government in a short-term capacity until I could see whether Madero would fulfill his promises to us.

Finally, I received orders to visit the villages that [the governor] had indicated along with the few people who still remained with me—thirty men—with the charge of removing the local authorities that the villagers disagreed with, and to prosecute the bandits.[33] I went to San Nicolás de Carretas, the place of my birth. I appointed authorities who reflected the wishes of the people. I went to San Lorenzo and did the same there. I went to many villages fulfilling my mission. I went to the village of La Joya, which also had difficulties with a leader imposed by Villa; I removed that leader and replaced him with one the people wanted.

I received an order from the governor to go to the village of San José del Sitio to see why the population had not allowed Captain Baca to enter along with twenty men. I then marched with sixteen men, and when I came close to the village, I sent a message to the mayor telling him that I had been sent to help the people resolve their difficulties, and to give them guarantees. The mayor replied that I would be allowed to pass. Upon my entrance, I was well received by all of the villagers.

I asked what difficulties the villagers had and why they had not allowed Baca to enter. They answered that the reason for not permitting him entry was the following;

—We had a mayor elected by the people, and we were satisfied with him. A few days ago, Baca came, dismissed our mayor on General Soto's orders, and replaced him with another one, whom the people do not want. Once Baca had left, we threw that mayor out of office and brought back the one we had chosen. Then Baca came back to dismiss our mayor once again. At that point, they told me that the people had decided not to let Baca enter. I told them:

—I am here on behalf of the governor to give you guarantees and provide justice to all those villages that need it. Your mayor will be the person whom you want.

And all of the villagers shouted with one voice:

—This is our mayor!

They introduced me to the man who was their mayor and told me:

—We are fighting for this: the liberty to elect our authorities.

—"Well done," I replied.

—"Long live Major Castillo, who came to bring us justice!" everybody shouted.

I validated their mayor, and the entire village was satisfied. On September 18, 1911, I left that village after completing my commission. All of the villagers accompanied me on my way out of the village. On my way back, I captured seven bandits in San Lorenzo in possession of fifty-two heads of cattle. I took them to Chihuahua City and handed them over to the authorities. Upon Villa's orders, the bandits were set free that same day, and the cattle was handed over to its rightful owners, who had followed us into the city.

I did not like the proceedings of the state government. I complained to the governor, telling him that we could not get rid of bandits that way and that it was not possible for Villa to defy the authorities for the sole reason that he thought of himself as a brave man:

—If you trust me, make me strong, and I will do away with this banditry. I am not scared of Villa. But once I bring [the bandits] to the authorities, don't let them go.

—"I don't know why they let these men go," the governor answered. "I will investigate why they were released, and I will give you one hundred men so that you can get rid of all of the bandits. You have done well in all of the villages you have visited; the villagers have written to me telling me that they are very grateful to you, and so am I."

MADERO RETURNS TO CHIHUAHUA DURING THE POLITICAL CAMPAIGN

I retired. [González] did not give me the hundred men that he had offered, and neither did he punish the accused. I continued to carry out my commission. In October, I received a telegram from the governor, asking me to go to [Chihuahua City] immediately with all of my men because Mr. Madero was arriving, and that I be there as an escort during his stay in Chihuahua.

I went to meet [Madero] at the train station. From that moment on, I understood from listening to Mr. Madero's words that he had no intention of fulfilling the promises that he had made to the people. His visit to Chihuahua had the sole purpose of making propaganda for [vice-presidential candidate José María] Pino Suárez. For that reason, [Madero and I] no longer saw eye to eye in Chihuahua.

[Madero] returned to Mexico City and took don Abraham with him so that he could take charge of the [Secretaría] de Gobernación.³⁴ Mr. Eduardo Hay, don Abraham, and several other people accompanied him on the return trip. Upon bidding me farewell, Mr. Hay told me:

—I always insist on you being with us in Mexico City. We are already taking don Abraham with us; let me know if I should make arrangements with Madero for you to go to Mexico City.

—Do as you please.

They left, and I marched to Cusihuiriáchic. Later, I received a telegram from the new [state] government, asking me to return immediately because the people in Mexico City were calling me urgently.

I went to Chihuahua City. I received two telegrams with urgent summonses for Ricardo Terrazas and myself. They told me that I should talk to my troops and ask them to elect someone to take my place as their chief while I was in Mexico City, a place where I did not think I would spend much time. The response of the soldiers was that they did not want another chief and that they would rather resign from the service, and all retired.

CASTILLO IN MEXICO CITY AGAIN

Terrazas, Valenzuela, my brother Apolonio, and I left for Mexico City. After we arrived, we went to Chapultepec and greeted Mr. Madero. He was surprised to see us and asked us:

—What are you doing here?

—We don't know, but you asked us to come.

—No, fellow, these are Hay's matters. He was the one who called you. Go see him and see where he will put you to work in Chapultepec Park. You are already here, so never mind.

We went to look for Mr. Hay and told him what Madero had said to us. —I wonder why he said that to you . . . [T]ell him when you see him next time that I will prove, along with don Abraham, that he [Madero] was the one who asked us to summon you here soon after our return from Chihuahua. Aboard the train, I pointed out to him that I wanted you to be here, and he told me to summon you as soon as possible. Don Abraham told him that it would be good if we did not call you too soon, since he had brought you there with the task of settling matters in several pueblos that were a bit disorganized, and that you had yielded good results. But [Madero] told him to replace you with someone else, because he also wanted you to be with him.

—Mr. Hay, we have come here because we have been summoned. I have already told you that I don't want employment for myself; what I would like Mr. Madero to do is to give me authorization so that they will pay me 1,300 pesos that I spent on the revolution. I gave a power of attorney to Mr. Santiago González, and he told me that a recommendation from Mr. Madero would be sufficient to obtain payment.

Then I told him:

—As far as those guys who are accompanying me are concerned: if you have any appreciation for their services, since you know that they suffered in the revolution on my side, I would like them to be given employment that can sustain their livelihood, because they are very poor. Just like me, they abandoned their work as railroad workers to rise up in the revolution, and it will be very difficult for them to get their jobs back, because the enemies of the revolution have continued to work there and will not want to rehire them.

—All right, Mr. Castillo, I will find them work with which they will be completely satisfied.

—Mr. Terrazas, how would you like to be chief of police here in Mexico City?

I saw that Terrazas blushed violently; he wanted to explode with anger, but thanks to the fact that he always took my interests into account, I was able to wink at him, and he obeyed me. After a few seconds, he replied:

—Mr. Hay; first of all, I am not used to serving as a policeman; and secondly, Mr. Castillo will return, and I will always stay at his side.

—Do as you please.[35]

We bade our leave from Mr. Hay and returned to Chapultepec several times to see if we would be able to speak to Mr. Madero. For twenty days, we waited at Chapultepec Castle from 7:00 a.m. to 5:00 p.m. Every day at 4:00 p.m., we greeted him when he left the castle, accompanied by his wife and the presidential guards. Every day I told him on the way out: "Sir, please grant me an audience, because I would like to talk to you for a moment."

—"Why haven't you come in?" he asked.

—Because they won't let me.

—Well, I will instruct them to allow you to enter the next time you come.

—I've come a few times, but I have not been able to talk to you, and there were important people waiting to speak to you, and I gave up.

—Are you already going to leave?

—Yes, sir.

—Well, go on then; you are both better suited for warfare. Don't let [General Bernardo] Reyes enter [the country], because he wants to come in through the border.

—I have still not been able to talk to you, as I desired.

—Well, then don't go just yet. Come back tomorrow so that we can talk, and so I can show you a horse that they brought from my hacienda . . . so that you can mount it to see if you like it.

We returned on Sunday at 6:00 a.m.; he was already out riding his horse. We stayed there until 11:00 a.m., without having had breakfast, and we tired of waiting for him and left without saying good-bye.

We went to Gobernación to bid farewell to don Abraham, and he told us:

—It's better if you don't go.

—We are more useful in our own homeland.

—In truth, I would also rather be there.

—Go back to where you were.

—But the War Secretariat has already dismissed us.

—These dismissals are not valid until I sign off on them, and I won't do so.

So we returned to Chihuahua to wait for the day when Mr. Madero would redistribute the land as he had promised. I waited in vain until February 5, 1912.

MÁXIMO CASTILLO JOINS THE ANTI-MADERO MOVEMENT IN CHIHUAHUA

I decided to join my dissatisfied comrades for several reasons. First of all, the majority of my comrades joined the revolution that broke out to demand the fulfillment of his promises from Mr. Madero. I also realized that my small contingent of eight to ten men could neither contribute to the resolution of the problems nor help my old comrades enforce the fulfillment of the Plan of San Luis; to wit, to carry out the redistribution of land to the laborers, as they had promised us. Finally, I knew I had not yet completely fulfilled my promise to fight to the death until the land, which existed in ample quantity, would be redistributed among the poor laborers.

On February 5, [1912,] I went to look for the revolutionary forces so that I could join them, and on February 7, I met them in Bachimba under the orders of Professor Braulio Hernández, who had already assembled a group of approximately two hundred men. That same day, we went to San Pablo Meoquí, where more people joined us.[36]

On February 8, José Orozco attacked us, capturing twenty prisoners and killing one of our men, and we took twenty of his troops. We disarmed them and let them go. Among the prisoners that they took from us was a brave first captain, Ricardo Terrazas, my faithful friend and longtime comrade-in-arms since 1910. That day, the professor withdrew toward Coyame, and in that pueblo, all the villagers joined us, and we advanced to Tres Castillos despite the bitter cold and the hunger. We carried neither blankets nor food. From Tres Castillos, we marched to Agua Nueva, and from there, to the station of Gallegos. We arrived at the station on March 1; and there we learned that General Salazar had risen up in revolt in Casas Grandes in the district of Galeana, and that he had already taken Cd. Juárez.

That same day, I served as courier to carry a message to General Salazar in Juárez. In this message, Hernández inquired whether the general agreed with our plans, and on the 4th, I left Juárez for Chihuahua

City in the company of General Salazar. On the same day, the forces of General Salazar and Professor Hernández combined, and we all marched toward Chihuahua City. That afternoon, we reached La Empacadora and made camp there. The chiefs did not want to enter the city until the next day, after Orozco had arrived to be sworn in as Supreme Chief of the Revolution.

THE PLAN OF LA EMPACADORA

At 10:00 a.m. on March 5, 1912, Orozco swore an oath on his life and the honor of his children to fight for the fulfillment of the Plan of Luis, as reformed in Tacubaya and Ayala. Afterward, all of the other chiefs and officers, including myself, swore the same oath and signed. Following this ritual, we entered the city to thunderous applause by the people, who thought that their desires had already been realized.[37]

Since I had the rank of major, Orozco awarded me the rank of lieutenant colonel on March 7, and I received the order to assume the command of the troops commanded by Professor Hernández. Immediately, I received orders to take a contingent of eighty troops to Santa Rosalía on March 11 under the command of General Salazar, who was going to attack the Federales in that village.

On the 12th, at 7:00 a.m., I got off the train close to the village. The general ordered a siege of the village and commanded me to attack the village from the south as part of the vanguard. I immediately marched with my troops to the center of the town, following the itinerary as instructed. The Federales had evacuated the town overnight and retreated to Jiménez, and [my superiors] gave me orders to pursue them immediately. Without giving us enough time to allow the horses to graze, which had not eaten for twenty-four hours, I pursued the Federales all the way to Jiménez. On March 14, at 7:00 a.m., I arrived in Jiménez, but the Federales had left in the direction of Parral by train four hours prior. I entered the fortifications without encountering any resistance; I took a prisoner and telegraphed General [Salazar] to let him know where the Federales had gone, as well as to request orders. I was told to stay there until further notice. On the 15th, the general came and told me that the Federales were in the station of Baca, and on the 16th, General Roque Gómez and I received orders to pursue them.

At 11:00 a.m. on March 17, we attacked them in the station of Baca. We forced them to retreat to the hacienda of Santa Cruz de Neira, where we captured forty prisoners. We laid siege to them until 6:00 a.m. the following morning, when they surrendered. They killed two of my men, and we killed five of theirs and wounded a few others. On this occasion, my troops distinguished themselves with their bravery; for example, First Captain Eleuterio Franco and all of the Coyame who were under my command. That same day—March 18—we rounded up the prisoners and took them to Jiménez. We stayed there until the 23rd, when I was ordered to come to the assistance of the comrades fighting at Rellano, where I arrived on the 24th. My help was no longer necessary because the battle was already over.[38]

I remained there until the 27th, when I was told to come to the assistance of those fighting in the small town of López, with the help of a train that they placed at my disposal. I immediately traveled to Jiménez, but my help there was not necessary, either, because [the Orozquistas] had already defeated the Federales under the leadership of Trucy Aubert. On April 5, I marched to Parral, at the orders of General Salazar, in order to attack Villa.[39]

At 11:00 a.m. on the 6th, we began the attack; and I received orders to attack from the south. I scaled a high mesa located there to be able to observe the positions of the enemy. We had not yet begun to figure out the layout of the village when they fired on us suddenly from two directions: the enemy held a position on a hill to my right, and on my left, on a few small, white hills, there was another enemy position. I sent my people to charge the position on the right, and within a few minutes, we had dislodged the enemy, which ran all the way back to the fortifications. We then moved on the position on the white hills. My men advanced, using the small hill and little streams as protection, until we were able to seize a cemetery at the base of the hills where the enemy was.

I was marching in the company of my old soldier, Juan Tapia. So that I would not go around it, I went straight through a plot of plowed land. When we were out in the open, the enemy opened intense gunfire on us that forced us to lie down on the ground. We spent a few minutes with the nose to the ground while the bullets whizzed over our backs, when Tapia told me:

—Get up, colonel, we will continue to advance . . . If they kill you, I will carry you on my back . . . [D]o not believe that I would leave you there. Words such as these, spoken by my good soldier, did not satisfy me, but they did oblige me to appreciate him to a greater degree. There was a moment when they stopped shooting at us, and we ran to the graveyard, where our other comrades had already stationed themselves.

At 6:00 p.m., we dislodged the enemy from their positions and entered the fortifications. I stayed there that night until noon the next day to help the general to establish order. Once that had been done, he ordered me to embark with all of my men in the direction of Santa Bárbara, already one league away from the village, so that we could make sure that the enemy would not come any closer.

Following my orders, I established my headquarters at that place and stationed my advance guard. I stayed there for five days while the general stayed in the fortification, accompanied by the other troops of his choice. They told me that he extracted ninety thousand pesos from that place, and every one of his officers took between two hundred and two to three thousand pesos. Since my troops did not have anything to eat, I asked the general for help, and he sent flour and jars filled with cold meat. We stayed there awaiting further instructions. We prepared to march once again, far away from his great estates, because it did not matter to us. We went to war to fight for the good of the poor people, and we did not seek fortunes to enrich ourselves.

General Salazar resented me, because I had been the one who guarded him in the station of Guzmán after he had been disarmed on Madero's orders.[40] At last, his disposition toward me softened due to my obedience and precise fulfillment of all of his orders. After that, we became good friends. He gave me good references with regard to my conduct, and whenever I wanted to fight, he ordered me to join the vanguard in the most difficult spot, and I did everything possible to carry out my orders. For that reason, he treated me a little better during the time that I served under his command.

THE DEATHS OF CANALES AND AMAYA

The regiments assembled in Jiménez. The honored and brave Colonel César Canales commanded the Eighth Regiment, and, due to the reports that he had read, he asked General Salazar to appoint me to his regiment as second in command. He got his wish.

Once our regiment was complete—meanwhile, the people from Coyame that I had brought had already been incorporated into another regiment—they commanded us to travel to the estates of Rellano, where we remained until May 7, when Colonel Canales received the order to march on Torreón with two thousand men. The Eighth Regiment under Colonel Canales's orders, which I had the honor of serving at the rank of lieutenant colonel, consisted of six hundred men. They ordered Generals Benjamín Argumedo, Emilio Campa, Juan B. Porras, and Colonel Abelardo Amaya to follow Colonel Canales's orders and march on Torreón as well. Although Colonel Canales was of lesser rank [than the three generals, he] was the chief of operations for our expedition.

On May 8, we left Rellano, and we took the municipality of Nazas on the 12th. During this first battle, I witnessed the colonel's bravery; and I believed that he would not last very long because he showed no fear whatsoever. When the assault began, he was in the middle of the street, ahead of everybody. I found myself obligated to accompany him among a rain of bullets. Without even noticing from where they were shooting at us, we arrived at the plaza, and a few minutes later, all of our men joined us. After half an hour of a battle, the enemy surrendered. We marched to Pedriceña, where we knew the enemy to be. On the 14th, we took Pedriceña. One of the first shots fired gravely wounded Colonel Canales, and a few moments later, Colonel Amaya was killed.

Canales had wanted to dislodge a group of enemy soldiers who were well ensconced on a railway bridge. He charged toward them without any cover whatsoever, and they felled him.[41] At that time, I was fighting another enemy group well ensconced on a small hill and a house that was serving as a hospital. After two hours of fighting, one of the assistants of the colonel came up to me and told me:

—The colonel wants to talk to you . . . [H]e is telling you to go over there.

I immediately ran to where [Canales] was. When he saw me, he told me:

—I asked to talk to you to give you my orders. My situation is grave, and I want to put my people under your charge; take care of them and follow the orders of General Emilio Campa.

—With great pleasure, my colonel, I will do all that you ask of me . . . [D]on't worry about the troops.

—"I am not worried," he replied. "I know well that I am leaving my soldiers in good hands; Providence will assist you."

—Colonel, I don't believe that you are in serious condition. God will be served if you recover soon. Right now, I will do the best I can to dislodge the enemy from the hospital, so that I can take you there and the doctor there can heal you.

—Ask Amaya to help you so that you can get the enemy out of there soon, so that you can take me there . . . [M]y relief depends on my swift recovery.

—I will go right now to ask them for a few soldiers.

He did not know that Amaya had been killed at the same time that he was injured.[42]

I continued to carry out the push necessary to dislodge the enemy from the hospital, but it was not possible to do so until 4:00 a.m. of the 15th. I took [Canales] to the hospital, but once the doctor saw him, he told me that it was hopeless. I left him with an escort of fifty men under the orders of the brave Captain Manuel Gutiérrez. I continued to fight the enemy, which attempted to retake the hospital with large numbers. At 8:00 [a.m.], the forces of Generals Argumedo, Campa, and Porras came to my assistance. Once they had arrived, we repelled the enemy, and we defeated them decisively on that same day, the 15th. At 3:00 p.m., my colonel died. Then I put myself under the command of General Campa as I had been ordered.

With the death of Colonel Amaya, the soldiers of the Fourth Regiment did not want to continue fighting, and on the 16th, [the regiment] returned to Chihuahua City. General Argumedo went to Zacatecas. Because of the departure of all of these troops, General Campa asked me what we should do with the small number of soldiers that remained with us. I gave him my opinion, which was to advance toward Torreón as we had been ordered to do. He agreed, and we marched toward Torreón.[43] I was ordered to march in the vanguard. When we got to a station of the railroad that runs from Torreón to Durango, a station named Guariáchi, I engaged in heavy gunfire with the enemy.

On the 17th, we came to the entrance of a canyon, and the general ordered me to send twenty troops as an advance party to see if there were enemy soldiers in the hacienda of Refugio, located at the exit of the canyon. If the enemy was not there, they were to pass by the hacienda toward the railroad and burn a few bridges, if possible, and then I was to take possession of the hacienda, where the general would join me the following day. I immediately sent the advance party as I had been ordered. They were under the command of Captain Cabada, and I then started marching with my remaining three hundred men out of the six hundred that had constituted the original Eighth Regiment.

On the next day, when I had already taken possession of the hacienda, I received a message from Captain Cabada that his men had destroyed a few bridges, but that the enemy had already begun to repair them. I sent him my dispatch [relating the events of the preceding day], because he was arriving with his troops. He ordered me to command Captain Cabada to inform us of the number of enemy troops, more or less. [Cabada] told us that there were six hundred to eight hundred men.

The following day, [May] 20, the general ordered me to send twenty more men to see if they could burn a bridge in the rearguard of the enemy, from where they were receiving reinforcements. I thought that my general did not have the will to fight, and since I saw that nothing could be gained by knowing how many enemy soldiers there were, or by burning bridges, I told him:

—If you will allow me, General, I will go with my troops to take a look at the enemy, and if I think that the right moment has come, I will attack them.

—"With much pleasure, go ahead," he replied.

Soon thereafter, I embarked on a rapid march along with one hundred troops that I had assembled. Since we knew where the enemy was, I looked for the best place from which to attack. I let the general know that I would attack the enemy at dawn on the 21st, and that he could send reinforcements if he wished. And indeed, I attacked the enemy forces at sunrise of the 21st. As I found out from a few prisoners that we captured, [the Federales] were under the command of Generals Peña and Morales Zaragoza. We defeated them on the 22nd. This two-day battle took place in a train station and a small ranch named España, according to our reports.

During the first day of the battle, First Captain Manuel Gutiérrez and his troops distinguished themselves by their bravery. Likewise, Captain Fabián Rico displayed the same degree of valor, and I asked General Orozco to promote both of them in rank because of their good conduct. Second Captain Juan Camacho attacked a bridge with sixty well-entrenched men and threw a bomb at them that sent them fleeing, scattering the group completely. Two of their bullets injured him as the bomb went off: one in the arm and the other, in the ribs. He fell to the ground and continued to fire at them. For this action, the captain was promoted that same day. The enemy fled, leaving in my possession seven engines with their respective wagons. I was just inspecting the trains when I received orders to assist the troops of General Campa. I ran to render assistance, but I soon received another message letting me know that [Campa's forces] had already repelled [the enemy]. Then I went to the hacienda La Loma, where General Campa was, to give him an account of my maneuvers.

I had hardly gotten to the hacienda around 9:00 a.m. when another message arrived from Captain Rico. He informed me that enemy troops were heading toward us in great number. I quickly ran to his meeting spot. A train full of Federales was on its way. In response, I stationed my troops on both sides of the road, on a few hills where the Nazas River makes a little estuary (an estuary by the name of España). The enemy arrived, put their artillery and machine guns into position, and we began to fight. Among the first gunshots, I captured a prisoner who informed me that the officer in command of his column was General Blanquet. His job was to come to the assistance of those whom we had already defeated.

DISORDER IN THE RANKS OF THE OROZQUISTAS

I was excited to hear that I would face off with the famous General Blanquet, and that so long as General Campa agreed to render me some assistance, I would have the opportunity to make him surrender and take him prisoner. Although I was not an ambitious person, I thought that it would look good if I captured a general as a prisoner.

For that reason, I sent a message to General Campa, who was stationed in the hacienda La Loma, one league away, with four hundred men. The message asked Campa to do me the favor of sending one hundred cavalry fighters to a small sierra just north of where I was fighting. This contingent was to stay hidden from the enemy, and it was to burn a bridge in the rearguard so that they could not escape. [General Campa] did not accede to my request. I continued to fight very much fatigued, running up and down the hills on foot, inspecting the positions of my troops under the scorching sun and without any water, so that my clothes made my sweat foam.

At noon, I sent another message to the general asking him (now in more brusque terms) to do me the favor of at least sending fifty useless troops that he had with him, but I did not get those, either.

General Pablo Ogaz, who was with me at that point, saw my agitation and said to me:

—If you would like, I will go with whomever I can find at this moment.

—Yes, please.

Shortly thereafter, he set out with fifteen troops that he had been able to assemble on short notice. But the enemy saw what was happening and sent one hundred dragoons toward him, preventing him from moving nearer to the railroad track. However, as soon as Blanquet saw our people on his flank, he reversed the train [and ordered his men to] rapidly load cannons and machine guns. The infantry that was unable to board the train on time ran like cowards. This happened at approximately 2:00 p.m. Because I could not get down from the hill on horseback quickly enough, I did not capture many prisoners; and at the beginning of the battle, my troops and I took those positions closest to us from the enemy. That day, I told my old soldier Tapia that I would ask General Orozco the next time I saw him to promote him to the rank of second captain in recognition of the bravery that he had demonstrated during the fighting.

Since the enemy had retreated, I remained in my positions. On the 24th, General Campa summoned me for a conversation at the headquarters. He had already retreated to the hacienda Refugio, two leagues from where my troops and I were stationed. He talked to me and proposed that we retreat to Durango or Chihuahua; as he pointed out, it was impossible to go ahead without any resources, as we lacked supplies and ammunition. I replied that I was under his command, and that he should dispose as he saw fit, but that I did not see any reason to retreat, since we were winning and had already made the enemy cede territory. To avoid difficulties with the troops, I suggested a meeting with my subordinate chiefs to ask their opinion about a possible retreat and march to Durango or Chihuahua.

That same day, I gathered my officers and came to an agreement with them. We decided not to retreat until we knew whether or not Salazar was approaching Torreón; if he were, we would make the greatest possible effort to draw closer to that city as well. We stayed there waiting for the enemy, regardless of the fact that General Torres and the majority of his troops had already left the area.

On the 2nd, I left with ten men on an expedition close to the station of Avilés. On the hillock of Rayo, I found an advance guard of the enemy, and we had a little skirmish. They were Blanquet's advance party returning with enough force to fight us. Once I saw the small number of people who were with us, as well as the low level of war materiel and ammunition and the impossibility of forging ahead or resisting the enemy, I gathered my officers to decide what we should do, and we agreed to return to Chihuahua to get word of the outcome of Orozco's battles and join the main part of the army. I had already heard that the Federales had chased Orozco out of Rellano and Salazar, out of Cuatro Ciénegas. Once we had come to this agreement, I told General Campa, and he gave his consent with pleasure.

We began to prepare our march, and we departed on the 29th with six gravely wounded comrades; without clothes to change into, food to give to them, or medications to help cure them. This trek of more than a month's duration, and through barren land that did not yield any sustenance, involved so many hardships that I had to take off my underwear so that they could give it to one of the wounded soldiers. I continued on wearing only my pants and jacket, naked otherwise.[xii] Like the other troops, who were barefoot and dying of hunger, I was covered with lice.[44]

xii. In the original, "a rais," which should be spelled "a raíz." This Mexican colloquialism connotes the lack of something, and Castillo is most likely referring to his lack of clothes. The term can also mean "barefoot," but in this context, this meaning is unlikely.

We finally reached Bachimba, where we found the main part of the [Orozquista] army. The great generals were in Pullman cars with elegant sleeping quarters and excellent kitchens with three or four cooks, with many different liqueurs to drink. Their troops were well dressed, with plenty of clothes and so many shoes that they could have sold some of them. Once they saw my tattered troops, they offered to sell them clothes and shoes because they had too many, and I immediately sent a telegram to General Orozco in Chihuahua City to inform him of the sad state of my troops. I was hoping to be able to travel to Chihuahua City in order to at least supply them with clothes. The reply was that I was to remain where I was until further notice, and that he would send me what my people needed. But he did not send me anything; or if he did, I did not get anything.

After three days, I received the order to march with my troops to Santa Rosalía, because the enemy was approaching. Right away, I marched on foot to the station of Conchos, while all of the generals and their troops traveled by train with all amenities. I immediately presented myself to General Salazar, who commanded me to proceed to La Cruz. He expected the arrival of the enemy: he had already sent Generals Rojas and Jesús José Campos, who returned with the news that the enemy was coming, but they did not put up any resistance. He ordered:

—Go ahead and meet up with the enemy to see what is going on, so that we know how many of them there are.

—I will do it with pleasure, although my drove of horses is in bad shape.

—Rest tonight, but leave by dawn and see where the enemy is coming from.

At seven in the morning, I left as I had been ordered. I had not even walked one kilometer when I encountered the enemy's advance party and began to shoot at them. When the generals heard the explosions, which could be heard well in the train station, they left with their troops to come to my assistance. We gathered the troops at the village of La Cruz, close to the main part of the enemy army. We fought them until 4:00 p.m.

General Salazar gave me the order to proceed through a small ravine that happened to be there until I was in position to take the first houses.

I carried out his command with twenty-five men who wanted to follow me. But once we came to the end of the ravine and approached the houses, the people who had followed me had already turned around. Only five soldiers remained with me, among them my brave old man Tapia, who never left my side no matter how grave the danger. There I was a mere twenty meters from the enemy: we fought all of them even though we were defenseless.[xiii] I remained calm because I heard rapid gunfire behind me and thought that it came from my comrades who were protecting me. But all of a sudden, General Salazar appeared next to me and told me: "Leave, colonel . . . [T]hey already have you surrounded . . . [O]ur troops have already fled." We quickly mounted our horses and escaped danger.

As General Salazar informed me, the enemy was already running away, but General Rojas, who had been ordered to outflank them on our right, got frightened upon seeing the fleeing enemy cavalry and ordered his troops to retreat. That was the reason why we did not completely defeat the enemy. I appreciate this action on the part of General Salazar, who had gone out to save me from the dangerous situation in which his orders had placed me. No other general would have done so.

We retreated to the station of Conchos. That night, all of the generals left by train with all of their troops without letting me know. My troops and I had been utterly exhausted from the walk and that day's battle, and we had not had a bite to eat. We had all needed to get some rest, and we were so dead tired that we had not noticed the departure of the trains.

I woke up at 1:00 a.m., and I was surprised to note the deep silence around me. It was still; there was no wind at all. I was afraid for the fifty or sixty troops who were with me. I feared that the enemy might have noticed the departure of the trains and come to attack me. I made my rounds through the encampment right away, and announcing to the troops that we were on our own.

We started moving. After dawn, we returned to Bachimba, where all of our forces were stationed. We were miserable as always; starving to death, naked, and covered with lice. We had not changed our clothes in two months.

xiii. In the original, "combatimos unos a otros a pecho descubierto."

On the day we arrived at Bachimba for the second time—and despite the order from above to stay there until further notice—I felt so sorry about the condition of my troops that I decided to travel to Chihuahua City to talk to General Orozco in person and plead with him to give me clothes for my troops. And I did so. After four days in Chihuahua City, I was able to speak to the general. He received me warmly and congratulated me on my victories in the Durango expedition and told me:

—You have the rank of colonel.

After a short conversation, I informed him of the miserable state of my troops. I was able to obtain a few clothes from him, but it was not enough for all of the soldiers.

But in these four days when I was in Chihuahua City, Major F. Rico despaired and marched to Chihuahua with sixty troops to make the same petition that I had just made. Because he had come without permission, he and his troops were disarmed, and he barely avoided the firing squad.

Thus we stayed in Bachimba until July 4, until we received new orders and retreated. I continued with my troops by land to the hacienda of Sauz, where we encountered General Orozco. There, he ordered me to Casas Grandes, where I would follow the command of General Salazar.[45]

THE DEFEAT OF OROZQUISMO

When I realized during my stay in Casas Grandes that Orozco had already betrayed our revolution, and that things were going very badly, there were moments when I considered retiring from the revolution. But in the end, I decided to keep fighting for my ideals, and to defeat the government in order to see if things would change.[46]

I was ordered to move on the hacienda of Ojito [*sic*] in order to attack the enemy that came from Sonora. Four hundred soldiers with artillery went there. These people went under my command as well as that of Colonel Alanís and other chiefs. On the first of August, we attacked the enemy and met with a resounding defeat. We returned to Casas Grandes, and from there, we marched back to Sonora under the command of General Salazar.[47]

At daybreak on September 13, we attacked El Tigre. At 3:00 p.m., they wounded my left arm; and at noon on the 14th, we took the fortification. From El Tigre, we set out toward Cananea. Near a mine by the name of Pilares, we joined up with the forces of General Rojas, and on the 19th, the enemy surprised us in a place called San Joaquín de Fronteras. When the enemy was already very close to us, General Salazar ordered me to go out to confront them.

I went out with ten men, thinking that all of the troops would follow me, but General Rojas was also issuing orders. He commanded his troops to run back to the rear to take control of some small hills that were very close to the encampment. I found the enemy and put up resistance for a moment, but they soon encircled me. Finding myself without any support from my other comrades, I ordered the ten troops with me to retreat, but to continue firing until we had returned to the location of our comrades. During our retreat, all of our horses got stuck in a swamp. The enemy captured two prisoners: Doctor Benjamín Aranda and a telegrapher by the name of González. Víctor Rincón Gallardo sustained serious injuries while hiding in a field of tall grass. My other comrades ran ahead, and I was trying to follow them even though I was completely spent, and too tired to walk, when two Yaqui Indians caught up with me. When they told me to stop, I fired a rifle shot at them, and they dropped down among the weeds. I went ahead, so fatigued that I repeatedly fell and needed to pick myself up again.

The first time I fell, my sombrero fell off my head, and I left it on the ground so as not to lose time, and they caught up with me. Farther ahead, the briars tore up my pants, and I did not pay them any notice. At last, almost dragging myself because of fatigue, I was able reach the positions of my comrades. After darkness fell, we retreated to Cananea, following the itinerary we had been given.

On the 20th, we slept near Agua Prieta. That night, General Salazar left without telling us. On the 21st, when we noticed that he had abandoned us, we gathered the troops so that we could choose a chief to replace General Salazar. Once together, all soldiers unanimously decided that I should take the command of the troops, and that they would continue to fight under my orders, and with pleasure. They also decided that we would return to the district of Galeana in the state of Chihuahua.

I told them that all of the chiefs and officers had made an agreement at the time of our departure from Galeana to Sonora to see where it was better to go to battle: in Chihuahua or Sonora. At the time, I had been the only one who thought that Chihuahua was better, because we knew the terrain and for many other reasons. But all others had expressed the opinion that we should go to Sonora, and I had readily consented. Now that we had barely set foot in the state of Sonora, I was ashamed to lead them back to Chihuahua. There was some opposition to doing so.

—I am going to ride my horse and charge ahead, but I won't tell you where we are going. Whoever wants to can follow me, and whoever does not want to, does not need to do so.

That is what I did. I put myself under the command of General Rojas, and we marched toward Cananea. All of the people from the district of Galeana, which had named me as their chief, returned [to Chihuahua]. Major Gutiérrez and Tomás Pérez went with me, two majors who had fought under my command and who appreciated me equally. So did their one hundred soldiers.

We joined General Rojas. Although I did not know him personally, I considered him a great general, brave and well intentioned. He was not the way I had thought, but he was a good friend and comrade. I was pleased to march with him during the month and a few days when we were waging revolution in Sonora.

A few days after joining up with General Rojas, we were close to the railroad to Agua Prieta when we saw a train coming. The general ran ahead and gave the order that twenty-five men should follow him; he was going to catch up with that train. I followed him with my troops to a watering trough that was located right there. I had ordered the killing of a cow, and the people were dismounting their horses when General Rojas returned, commanding us to take to the ridge of a nearby sierra because the enemy was arriving in large numbers. We followed his orders right away and followed him, because he was walking ahead of us. When we were already on the crest of the sierra, we noticed that several soldiers on the train got off. We sent some shots their way, and they scattered.[48]

That night, we slept in the summit of that sierra by the name of Sierra de los Ojos, without eating dinner. We had not had lunch, either. We could see Cananea from there: one could make out the beautiful lighting at the mine. At daybreak on the 22nd, we received orders to march on. We did so on top of the sierra. We walked all day, and at dusk we found some cattle. We felled two of them, and we had not even begun to make a fire, let alone roast a chunk of meat, when we were told to march on immediately. I went to see the general to find out why we had to leave so suddenly. I told him that the troops and the horses were very tired and hungry. He told me that he had just received notice that the enemy was pursuing us in great number, and that they were in the process of encircling us. We needed to continue on our way.

There was nothing we could do, and we left right away. We walked most of the night, and at dawn, we received the same order to march and reach high ground because they were pursuing us. The general received these messages in the small ranches we happened upon along the way, and so he kept marching us day and night over the sierras for twenty-two days.

On October 10, fed up at last with the constant marches day and night and without necessities, we decided to return to Chihuahua. I told [General Rojas] that we were going to Chihuahua because we could not do anything [in Sonora] because we did not know the terrain, and that there was danger everywhere because there were so many enemy troops. We were not fighting them but, instead, fleeing through the sierra.

—Comrades, if you are going to Chihuahua, I will accompany you.

So we returned to Chihuahua. When we left Sonora and arrived at the border of the state of Chihuahua, the general decided to go attack the hacienda of San José de Babícora to obtain our necessities. We knew that this hacienda had what we needed, but fifty to one hundred armed men stood guard to protect it.

We went to the hacienda, and when we arrived, [General Rojas decided that] it was no longer worthwhile attacking it. Then he suggested an attack on San Pedro Madera instead, which had little protection. We approached San Pedro Madera from the east. We burned a few bridges and seized an engine that was making movements. In a train station by the name of El Rincón, he decided not to attack San Pedro and ordered us to destroy the Central railroad line as well as seize a train full of supplies. We marched through the Central to the hacienda of San Gerónimo de Almeida, where the enemy surprised us on November 6.

No matter how hard the other chiefs and I fought to resist the enemy, we could not do it. The general ordered the [remaining] troops to retreat to the ridge of a nearby sierra. When we came to the first small hill, I stopped with fifteen or twenty men whom I was able to hold up, and we awaited a large group of enemies who pursued us. We repelled them, forcing them to return to the hacienda. Once the enemy had retreated, we continued on top of the sierra in search of the general with the majority of the troops. We found him at the highest point of the sierra with his men in position, waiting for the enemy.

CASTILLO JOINS THE FORCES OF MARCELO CARAVEO

When we realized that the enemy was no longer pursuing us, we continued our march in the direction [of Chihuahua], making detours around the villages along the way for fear of enemy soldiers. When we were attacking a few small ranches, we got notice from General Caraveo, who was in Nido Canyon with a group of troops. Caraveo had already had three encounters with the enemy, and he had already taken Palomas. We went to the canyon in search of Caraveo, and indeed, we found him there. Immediately upon our arrival, we put ourselves at his service and named him superior chief of all the generals, colonels, and officers united there.

On December 2, General Caraveo ordered us to attack a defensive position in the station of Laguna, to see if we could seize a train loaded with supplies. I got the commission to attack the guards in the station and to station my troops in strategic locations during the night. The next day, I was to let the passenger train pass, only to seize it in the station of Mocho. I carried out the order that I had been given and stationed my troops in a hidden location close to the station. On the 3rd, the train came through at 9:00 a.m. Once the train had departed, we attacked the station, and within one hour we had forced the enemy to surrender. We killed three of their men and took fifteen prisoners. Generals Caraveo, Rojas, and Porras boarded the train and defeated the escort that was aboard; they took the provisions that they found, and we went back to the Nido, where our headquarters were.

On the 12th, General Salazar arrived at our camp and invited us to join him in taking the village of Ascensión. He said he had some troops, and that together with ours, they would be able to take Ascensión and its garrison of three hundred men. With pleasure, we all agreed to join him.[49] General Caraveo handed over the post of supreme chief to General Salazar, and on the 13th, all of us marched under Salazar's orders. On the 20th, we took the fortification of Ascensión and marched to the hacienda of Ojitos.

On the 24th, we learned that the enemy was approaching, and on the 25th, we went out to confront them at the fortification of Janos. I went to the right, Generals Rojas and Porras took the middle, and Generals Salazar and Caraveo went to the left. We fought all day. At 4:00 p.m., I forced the enemy to retreat on the side where I was. Unfortunately, at the same time, the enemy dislodged Generals Rojas and Porras at the center of our forces, and Salazar and Caraveo also retreated. I did not notice what was occurring at these other positions. I heard loud gunfire, but I thought that my comrades were repelling the enemy just as I had done. I continued to fortify my positions until the night, when I received a message from Salazar telling me to retreat, since they had already done so and were awaiting us in Ojitos. I received the notice with surprise, since I thought that all of us had defended our positions. At 9:00 p.m., I retreated to the hacienda of Ojitos, where the generals and all of the troops were.

On December 12, 1912, in the vicinity of the neighborhood of Pacheco, the enemy attempted to prevent our passage through the hacienda of San Pedro. We had a little skirmish during which they killed one of our colonels and injured one of our soldiers. We went ahead to the Pacheco neighborhood. There, General Rojas, Colonel Roque Gómez, and I received orders to go and attack the valley of San Buenaventura.

THE OROZQUISTAS CAPTURE JOSÉ DE LA LUZ BLANCO

We marched following our orders, and on January 7[, 1913], we encountered the forces of General Blanco on our way through San Miguel Babícora. It was the coldest day of my life. Amid the cold snow, we fought until we captured General José de la Luz Blanco. But General Rojas was so surprised when he saw the prisoner that he gave the order for all of us to pull back, firing [at the enemy] during the retreat. I pleaded with him repeatedly not to give ground: why retreat if we were winning? But it was not possible to convince him; he ordered the pullback and left with the prisoner and several people who accompanied him.[50] At that time, I was already attending to First Captain Juan Camacho, who had been shot in the head. When I was free, I ordered Captain Patrocinio Ontiveros to tell our men not to vacate their positions. I had unsaddled one horse and was in the process of saddling another when the captain approached and told me:

—Sir, I gave the order, but all of the people are already coming . . . [O]ne of them is going around telling everyone that General Rojas gave the order to get up and follow him.

When I heard that, I said:

—Well, if all of the troops are already coming back here, there is nothing else we can do; let's follow the general.

At that very moment, a bullet struck Captain Ontiveros in the shoulder; the impact was so weak that it hardly emerged on the other side. The bullet was stuck between the vest and the jacket. For that reason, we followed the general, thinking that all of our men had already retreated from their positions. I did not notice twenty to twenty-five men who remained in their positions until the enemy encircled them. Fifteen of them died.

We continued toward the valley of San Buenaventura, and when we reached the canyon of San Joaquín, we noticed footprints of about three hundred troops marching ahead of us. In the ranch of the same name, we found out that the footprints came from the men of Generals Salazar and Caraveo, who had passed the day before on their way to the valley. We sent out a scout team to find them, and they found them on a ranch two leagues from the valley.

When General Salazar got word that we were in San Joaquín, he ordered an attack on the valley. That night, he sent a message to General Rojas instructing him to advance immediately to come to his assistance. General Rojas replied that he would start moving at 3:00 a.m. with his troops, and that he would arrive there by daybreak. Then, General Salazar ordered General Caraveo to begin the attack with two hundred men, and that General Rojas would join him at dawn.

That night, General Blanco's troops came as reinforcements from the valley in which we had fought at San Miguel de Babícora. General Caraveo did not notice the arrival of these troops. Caraveo's men attacked and conquered two headquarters of the enemy, but [the Federales] realized that the number of their attackers was small and hence put up stiff resistance. Once General Caraveo realized that no reinforcements were on their way, he realized that he had to retreat.

Indeed, General Rojas, who had offered [General Salazar] to move out his troops at 3:00 a.m., had not done so until 7:00 a.m. Since I knew that we had promised to get moving at 3:00 a.m., my troops and I were ready at that time. At 3:00 a.m., I began to move the troops out of some of the camps, but the general was asleep, and it was useless. Eager to come to the assistance of my comrades who were fighting, at 6:00 a.m., my people and I went without waiting for the general. Before we had walked one mile, however, an emissary from the general caught up with me and ordered me to stop until he got there with all of the remaining troops. He arrived at 9:00 a.m. and ordered me to march in step with the infantry.

At 10:00 a.m., we arrived at the ranch where they were waiting for us. To speed things up, Salazar came out to meet us. Since I was walking ahead with the vanguard, he told me:

—Run to give support to Caraveo . . . [S]ince last night, he has been fighting in the valley.

I galloped with twenty to twenty-five men who had the best horses. When we got to the first houses, we happened upon Caraveo, whom [the enemy] had already driven out of the village. There, the two generals agreed that they would no longer attack this fortification because they knew that the enemy was about to receive reinforcements in the number of one thousand men. From there, we marched toward the ranch of Sanguijuela in the municipality of Ahumada.

The generals decided to divide up the troops to facilitate the procurement of provisions. General Caraveo went to Carmen; and Salazar, to the hacienda of San Luis. While there, I found out that my brother, Apolonio, was looking for me along with twenty of his men. They were camped out in Nido Canyon, and I sent a soldier to look for him. I desired to see him because it had been seven months since we had been separated, and I had always proceeded very carefully because I did not know what had happened to him. On July 29[, 1912], I had sent him on a commission to Cd. Juárez, and he had not been able to rejoin us because of the destruction of the Ferrocarril del Noroeste.

I was so overjoyed at the news about my brother that I told the man whom I was sending to find him not to return unless he came back in his company. I continued the march with General Salazar to the village of Carrizal. The two generals had agreed to meet to attack Villa Ahumada, four leagues away from that village. We got to [Carrizal] on the day when Caraveo was supposed to be there as well. But that general did not do what he had agreed to do; he returned to Chihuahua City from the hacienda of Carmen.

The enemy found out in Villa Ahumada that we had arrived in Carrizal. They sent ten men to reconnoiter; of the ten, we took one prisoner, and the other nine ran away. General Salazar, Major Manuel Gutiérrez, and I pursued them almost all the way to the town. After our return, during a moment when the general and I were alone, he told me that he no longer knew what to do, or even what to think about continuing the revolutionary cause. He asked me what we should do with the troops: naked, barefoot, infested with lice, and without food or even the prospect thereof. Caraveo had not returned; he had gone in a different direction. [As the general thought,] everyone had begun to scatter.[51] He begged me to do him the favor of summoning the chiefs, General Rojas, and the other colonels and officers to decide what we should do and so that they could share their point of view.

That same night, I got everyone together, and I began by telling them the purpose of our meeting. We began to exchange our points of view. Colonel Roque Gómez was the first who shared his opinion. He said that we should seek amnesty under good guarantees because there were no more revolutionaries except ourselves as far as he could see. I responded to this proposition as follows:

—Gentlemen, it is not honorable for us, who are revolutionaries with ideas, to seek amnesty of any kind; rather than that, I would prefer to die of starvation in a sierra or to go to the great country of China.

I told them that I was sure that there were other revolutionaries farther south in addition to ourselves, and that the reason why we did not know of their existence was that we had not been able to read the press for more than six months. I was sure that the revolution had not ended, and that we were not alone, and I thought we should draw closer to the border to look at the press and orient ourselves; there, we could get good information about the situation. Once we had that information, we should consider what to do next. All of them agreed with my opinion, and we told General Salazar what we had agreed on. He shared our opinion and immediately ordered us to march on the village of Guadalupe near the borderline.

When we got to the village, some of our partisans who lived in Texas came to join us. They brought information about the state of the revolution. Upon reading the press, we found out that there were revolutionaries in the south of the republic. Zapata stood tall in the state of Morelos. One of those who came was the engineer David de la Fuente, a revolutionary and comrade who lived in Texas. General Salazar suggested to him that he call upon the *licenciado* [Emilio] Vázquez Gómez to head a provisional presidency and put himself at the head of the revolution.[52]

We left Guadalupe in the direction of Puerto Palomas to wait for the *licenciado*, whom they had summoned from San Antonio. When we were in Guadalupe, the general was conferring with representatives of the [federal] government. I never knew what was going on during those negotiations, but a rumor circulated among the soldiers that the general was seeking amnesty. That's what one of the soldiers told me. I did not believe that rumor and sought to counteract it by telling them that it could not be true. Even if it were true—I told them—I was not ready to seek amnesty. Instead, I would desert and hide out in a sierra until things changed—and if any of my comrades wished to follow me in that event, I would be happy to include them.

I told General Rojas about these rumors and shared my line of thinking with him. He replied that he thought the same way, and that he had not told anyone else. Since he and I thought along the same lines, he said, we could go fight with the Yaqui rebels [in Sonora]. We embraced and shook our right hands and swore that we would not recognize any government other than one that emanated from the revolution of the Plan de San Luis, as amended in Tacubaya and Ayala.

General Salazar's orders in Puerto Palomas included destroying the bridges of the [Ferrocarril del] Noroeste from Pearson to Cumbre. I was to return without fail on February 25, 1913. On the 7th, I left to fulfill this commission. After I had destroyed a few bridges, I took a freight train originating in San Pedro Madera, and the conductor showed me a telegram that he had intercepted. The telegram stated that there was fighting in Mexico City, and that Félix Díaz had already taken the armory [of that city]. After hearing this news, I stopped blowing up bridges and returned to Palomas to render an account of my commission.

On my way back, I passed through San Miguel de Babícora. I visited the place where we had fought the forces of General Blanco when he fell into our hands. There, I found the bodies of fifteen of our comrades strewn all over, dismembered by wild animals. With their faces so toasted by the sun and snow that they looked like Africans, they were hardly recognizable. They had lain there for a month and seven days. In all of the revolution, I had never come upon such a scene. I ordered them buried and continued on my way. On the 24th, I returned to Puerto Palomas. I rendered the dispatch of my commission, and then the general introduced me to *licenciado* Vázquez Gómez and placed him in my care, as I would be serving as his guard. I learned that Huerta had overthrown Madero in a military uprising.

A few days later, we found out that they had killed Madero and Pino Suárez. [Vázquez Gómez] expressed his opinion by saying:

—Have you heard the news of this despicable treason?

A flash of indignation shot through my mind as I pondered the news of the assassination. Huerta had not only dishonored the Mexican army, but the entire nation. "What will all the nations of the world think of the Mexicans?" Then I thought that our situation would become a lot more difficult, and that the triumph of our cause would be delayed during the shedding of more and more brotherly blood.

I passed the time worrying until we learned that Huerta had invited all revolutionaries to join him, and that he was on the side of the revolution and had the best intentions to fulfill its ideals. When Orozco, who was living in hiding in El Paso, Texas, found out what was happening in Mexico City, he left his hiding place to join Huerta. He recognized

[Huerta] as the supreme chief of the entire revolution and its only representative.[53] Once Orozco and Huerta were united, General Salazar remained firm for a few days, unwilling to make an alliance with the traitors. For that reason, I continued to follow him with great pleasure.

At that point, my brother Apolonio arrived at our camp. It had been more than six months since I had heard from him. He had allied himself first with Caraveo and then with Orozco, who had already emerged from his hiding place and was asking the revolutionary groups to submit themselves to his command so that he could represent the revolution in the north. Orozco sent my brother to go wherever he might find me with the pretext of saying hello, and with the real purpose of asking me to desert from General Salazar and to accompany him to Mexico City, where Huerta was. He would take great pleasure in my joining them so that I would not have made in vain the great sacrifices for our cause.

I received my brother with great happiness, because not knowing his fate had caused me great anguish. After telling me about his adventures and the great dangers of his campaign in the south of the republic, among people whom he did not know, he told me of the commission that Orozco had given him. Once I knew what it was, I told him:

—Brother, luck wished that we would reunite. Neither you nor I will go where Orozco is going. I will never recognize a government that has tarnished the honor of the entire nation with its treason. It is better to lose [the benefit of] all of the sacrifices that we have made and remain in oblivion than to stain our own honor. We need to remain firm in our ideas; better to die than to appear as traitors before history. Huerta is not a part of the revolution; and even if he were, he would betray it upon his triumph, just like he betrayed and assassinated the president. He would continue to assassinate all of the revolutionaries who have fought for the redistribution of land.

After the end of the conversation with my brother, I went to the headquarters. There, *Licenciado* Vázquez Gómez and General Salazar had agreed to send a representative . . . to Mexico City to settle issues pertaining to the revolution. They had decided on the engineer David de la Fuente due to his honesty and talent, and because he had sacrificed himself for our cause. Once in Mexico, this gentleman had to settle for a post as a gift from Huerta. He sent telegrams to General Salazar informing him that everything had been sorted out, and that he should immediately take his troops to Casas Grandes to assume the position of district chief of Galeana. Vázquez Gómez was to withdraw his claim to the provisional presidency and retire.

THE RELATIONSHIP WITH EMILIO VÁZQUEZ GÓMEZ

General Salazar received those telegrams in the station of Guzmán. He quickly marched to Casas Grandes, following his orders, and sent a telegram to Palomas in order to inform the *licenciado* [of de la Fuente's instructions]. He sent another order to me to gather my troops in Casas Grandes.

When I learned that I had received the order to summon my troops to Casas Grandes, and that my general had already subjected himself to the Huerta government in a betrayal of our ideals, I tore up the order impatiently. "I am not going . . . I am not a traitor." I consulted with [Vázquez Gómez] and asked him to give me his opinion. I told him that I was not in agreement with what was happening at the moment, and that I would never be willing to submit myself to a treasonous and murderous government such as Huerta's.

—*Licenciado*, you know that I subscribed to the Revolution of 1912 to demand of Mr. Madero the fulfillment of the Plan of San Luis as subsequently amended at Tacubaya and Ayala. Do me the favor of letting me know what I should do, and if you are willing to support me, give your orders to my troops and me.

He responded with some emotion:

—Mr. Castillo, go where your general has sent you; I am thinking of resigning, even though I believe that Huerta will not fulfill the ideals of the revolution. It is possible, however, that he will; and if it is true that we are continuing to sacrifice ourselves for our fatherland, we need to sacrifice our own person on its behalf. So go where your general has commanded you; you and I will stay in touch, and I will let you know what we need to do.

I obeyed the order of the *licenciado* so as not to annoy him. I thought that I would go where I had been told to go, but that I would not remain a single additional minute under the orders of President Huerta, nor would I hand over my troops, nor resign immediately.

The *licenciado* withdrew to the United States, and I marched to Casas Grandes. None of my soldiers was in agreement. We arrived at the headquarters, and I rendered my dispatch as usual. At that moment, I shared my disagreement with the general and asked him to accept my resignation and discharge. No matter how much I pleaded, I was not able to convince him. I returned five days later and told him:

—Do me the favor of accepting my resignation and discharge, because I wish to see my family, which is suffering horribly without resources of any kind . . . My son does not have work . . . I want to go at all costs to see how I can remedy the needs of my family. In addition, I am tired of fighting and risking my life without any benefit for our cause.

He roundly refused to accept my resignation.[54]

—If it is not possible for you to accept my resignation, then at least give me permission to go see my family.

—That is something that I will be able to do; I can give you leave for three or four days.

I left General Salazar under this pretext. When I said good-bye to my comrades, I informed them that I was leaving and would not return. I told them:

—You all know what you are doing. If I cannot continue fighting for our sacred cause, I had better stay over there in the United States. Those of you who would like to follow the general, do so; and those who do not want to follow him, take your leave and ask for your discharge. The only thing I have to tell you is that it is not honorable to recognize an unworthy government such as this one.

Major Gutiérrez answered me:

—My colonel, I don't agree with Huerta and even less with being his soldier, and the majority of our troops also disagree. If you leave, I will, as well, and if you continue to fight for the cause, I will enjoy accompanying you. I believe that all of the people who have fought with you will follow us without hesitation.

—All right, I will go, then, and when I am in El Paso, I will let you know if I can arrange something good for our cause. I will tell you what you need to do; and I will always give you a heads-up so you can think about it and proceed as you wish.

Once I had arrived in El Paso, I found out that Vázquez Gómez was also there. I talked to him regarding our commitment to the revolution. He told me that he had finally decided not to withdraw his claim to the provisional presidency. Zapata, he said, had fought for the Plan of Ayala and Tacubaya, and that he [Vázquez Gómez] was willing to support Zapata. If I wanted to support the revolution in the north in accordance with the ideals of the south, he added, I would be the one who continued to carry the flag of principles.

I answered:

—With much pleasure, because I have suffered for those ideals, and I have sworn on my honor as well as that of my children to fight until death or victory. You know it, *Licenciado:* give me your orders.[55]

—Very well, continue holding up our flag; the triumph of our cause is drawing near.

He awarded me the rank of brigadier general.[56] It was a surprise to me. Afterward, I went to visit the other political supporters to confer with them in order to come to an agreement regarding the new movement. I talked to don Paulino Martínez, Professor Braulio Hernández, and many other supporters.

CASTILLO SEEKS A CONNECTION WITH EMILIANO ZAPATA

Don Paulino showed me a letter signed by General Zapata. In that letter, [Zapata] asked whether the revolution of the north had ended completely, and he sent his regards to the *licenciado* Vázquez Gómez. We agreed to answer General Zapata and tell him that the revolution of the north had not died entirely, but that I was continuing it with a small group of comrades. We told Zapata that I was at his service.

I issued a manifesto on April 24, 1913, to let the world know the principles of my revolution. I wrote to Major Manuel Gutiérrez to let him know that I was entering the revolution once again, and that he should break away from Salazar with all of the men who wanted to follow him. I told him that we would see each other quite soon in the sierra of Capulín.

On May 3, I crossed the border in Puerto Palomas. I issued another manifesto inviting all of the contending factions to join together in the flag of principles, either with me or with the southern forces of General Zapata. There, I found out that Major Gutiérrez had broken away from Salazar with three hundred men, and that he had already seized the valley of San Buenaventura, where he was waiting for our arrival. I went to the valley, and they put themselves at my service. I ordered them to proceed to Puerto Palomas, where we would prepare ourselves to commence our operations.

On the way to Palomas, I met with Salazar in the station of San Pedro. At that meeting, we talked about the reason for my decision to break away and about the ideals that we had defended. He invited me to join Huerta, which I could not accept. He told me that he was fighting for the same ideals as I was, and that his alliance with Huerta had the objective of finding the resources necessary to sustain the revolution. If I agreed to join them, he said, he would return to the battlefield along with me once he had secured enough materiel from the government. His promise did not satisfy me, but we agreed that our forces would not fight each other.

We drew up a report to document what we had agreed upon and finished our discussion.[57]

Then I talked to Lieutenant Colonel Duarte, a follower of General Antonio Rojas, who came with the task of conferring with me on behalf of General Rojas. He made me the same proposition that Salazar had already made. He showed me a letter from Rojas in which he made mention of our embrace in Guadalupe, where we had sworn on our word of honor not to recognize any government that did not emanate from the revolution. The letter stated that [Rojas] had recognized Huerta for the same reasons as Salazar, and that he would soon return to the battlefield of the revolution; he was ready to fulfill his vows and would see me soon on the field of honor. I answered him that he had already broken his word, but that he would be well received if he returned to my side one day to fight for our principles.

After this meeting, I continued on to Puerto Palomas. I procured supplies and began operations. My subordinates and I agreed to attack Pearson, the location of one hundred garrisoned Federales. I went to Pearson, and we took it. The attack began at 3:00 a.m., and at 7:00 a.m., the enemy surrendered. We had killed eighteen and captured eighty prisoners; among the dead, we found the chief of the garrison, a colonel. I took one hundred rifles and eighteen thousand cartridges from them.

THE LAND REDISTRIBUTIONS AND CONFRONTATIONS WITH VILLA

I got word that Villa was advancing from San Andrés to Casas Grandes. I thought that Villa was on my side, as Professor Hernández reported after hearing Villa say so on his way out of El Paso. I therefore ordered my troops to blow up the bridges north of Juárez so that Salazar, who was in Chihuahua City, could not come to the assistance of [the Federales] in Casas Grandes. Thus Villa would be able to take that fortification easily.

After capturing Pearson, I went to the hacienda of San Diego. I divided up the hacienda and the harvest among the peons and share-croppers. Then I went to Terrazas's other haciendas and split them up in the same fashion. In the hacienda of San Lorenzo, I learned that Villa was already in San Pedro Madera, advancing on Casas Grandes. I sent him a message along with my communications and manifestos and told him that I wanted to know if we were in agreement or not. He neither answered nor returned my message.[58] As a result of this behavior, I suspected that [Villa] did not agree with my ideals, and that it would be difficult to come to an understanding. I already knew too much about his bad conduct.

I continued to parcel out land to poor farmers. I divided up six of Terrazas's hacienda, as well as one belonging to the Miller family. I visited several villages and told the inhabitants that we were the standard-bearers for the redistribution of land. I read them the deeds of the haciendas that had been parceled out and thus proved that I was fighting for the good of the poor.[59] After showing them the force of my cause, I invited those who wanted to fight for the good of our poor brothers to accompany me so that soon, all of the poor would have a small plot of land of their own with which they could sustain their children. They very much liked the work that I was doing, but they did not accompany me because they realized that there was only a small number of us, and they did not believe that Zapata, in the south, and I could dominate the situation. They believed that public opinion was on the side of the Constitutionalists or of Huerta, except those Constitutionalists who had the support of the United States.

In the valley, I received more news: Villa had taken Casas Grandes and was stationed in Ascensión with 1,500 men, and a few of Salazar's dispersed troops wanted to join up with mine. After hearing the news, I sent one hundred men to Casas Grandes under the command of Lieutenant Colonel José Parra to see if it was indeed possible to gather those dispersed soldiers. Meanwhile, I marched to Villa Ahumada with two hundred troops in order to capture its fortifications, which were guarded by a small group of Huertistas under the command of Colonel Enrique Portillo. When [Portillo] found out that I was drawing near, he evacuated the town and went to Cd. Juárez.

Once Villa realized that this small contingent of mine was stationed in Casas Grandes, he sent a force of five hundred men to attack them. He surprised them and defeated them. They captured Lieutenant Colonel Parra and his son, First Captain Alfredo Parra. He shot both and thus confirmed the distrust that I had always had of him, and I was now convinced that he was my enemy. I learned of the defeat of my comrades upon my return to the hacienda of San Luis.[60]

Then I marched to the community of Pacheco. I set up my headquarters there for a few days, gathering the dispersed troops on their way to the community of Pacheco. In a ranch called La Fragua, an emissary of Salazar, Mr. Ramón Chacón, caught up with me. He told me that Salazar and other generals had commissioned him to confer with me. I authorized my secretary to answer whatever questions Mr. Chacón might have. Once the questions had been asked, and answered by my secretary, we drafted a summary of the conference. Mr. Chacón left, and I went to Pacheco.

I reincorporated a few dispersed soldiers of my force [that had gone to Casas Grandes], but the defeat that they had suffered had greatly demoralized them. They told me that they did not think that Villa was our enemy, and some of them began to desert; a few, to Villa, and others, to Salazar. They believed that Villa and our group were fighting for the same party, and that it was best for them to join Villa because he was stronger and had a greater chance of victory because the North Americans protected him.

While I was there, I regrouped a total of sixty troops of my force who had been dispersed, among them two majors, Timoteo Marrufo and

Benigno Tarín, whom I had already observed as making propaganda among the troops to desert to Salazar. Induced by them, some had already deserted. At last, I was able to find a letter from Enrique Portillo that recommended to them that they should leave me and join him. They had already told them that they would leave [my forces], and they continued to work in order to take as many people with them as they could.

Once we had discovered that they were making propaganda and found the letter, I ordered their detention. They were court-martialed for this crime, as well as for ordering the murder of a Chinese national who had refused to give them five pesos as they had asked. The court-martial sentenced them to execution by firing squad. Despite the executions, it was not possible to stop the desertions.

From there, I went to take San José de Babícora at 6:00 a.m. with one hundred people I had left. We fought all day and night, and it was not possible to capture the hacienda due to its good fortifications and our lack of grenades. We set fire to the doors where they were stationed, but the pouring rain did not permit them to burn.

I retreated and visited the haciendas where we had redistributed the land, asking the people to give away their share of the harvest so that they could remedy the needs of their children. It became necessary to ask them by force. They did not want to give away their share even though they were used to giving it up every year.[61]

THE RUPTURE BETWEEN MÁXIMO CASTILLO AND BRAULIO HERNÁNDEZ

I returned to Puerto Palomas and established my headquarters there with my few remaining troops. At that time, the manager of the company of the hacienda of Nogales came to my camp in order to arrange the shipping of a herd of cattle to the United States.

Professor Braulio Hernández, a professor and comrade who deserved my complete trust, made an arrangement with the manager of the company, taking advantage of his good English. The arrangement stipulated that the manager would use his influence with the other companies to recognize [Hernández] as the supreme chief of the revolution in the north, as well as the provision of a loan of five hundred thousand dollars. In exchange for this sum, he assured [the North Americans] that he would give full guarantees, and that their haciendas and interests would not be damaged at all in the future. Even afterward, in a state of peace, the lands would not be parceled out like all of the others.[62]

Once I had been informed of the arrangements that [Hernández] intended to make, probably with the sole purpose of making a great profit under the pretext of revolution, I saw myself forced to sever ties with him even though I appreciated him very much personally. As soon as the professor had split from our group, I continued to operate with the few troops that I had left. I made an effort to increase their number, but it was impossible: other armed troops feared joining me because the enemy was very powerful, and I did not hold out much hope that they would change their mind.

Meanwhile, Villa sent me frequent messages asking for a meeting—a meeting that I never wanted to have with him. One day, Major Miguel Samaniego approached my camp, the chief of a small group of Carrancistas. He invited me to a meeting, an invitation that I accepted with pleasure. We had two meetings that yielded no results: we could not agree on a common strategy. He tried hard to make me join the Constitutionalist movement, and I invited him to join my party: my cause was just and one of principles, whereas the Plan of Guadalupe did not promise anything else except to restore the government of Francisco I. Madero. One time when we had a disagreement, he asked me not to escalate our antagonism in view of our common aim of seeking the overthrow the Huerta government. I accepted that proposition, and we ended our discussions.

A few days after this conference, Villa's wife passed through my encampment accompanied by three young ladies. This lady had no choice but to arrive at my encampment, as she did not know that I was in Puerto Palomas, [a town] through which she had to pass to reach [the United States]. I treated her with decency, just as one should treat all of the families. I escorted her to the border with ten men to make sure that my soldiers would not bother her, and I asked her to let her husband know that I knew how to treat the families of my enemies. The lady expressed her gratitude and offered to tell her husband of the kindness with which I had treated her. I later found out that both spouses were grateful. In fact, once Villa took Chihuahua City, he confiscated my house but returned all of my property in appreciation of my kindness toward the lady.

In February 1914, I established my headquarters in Pearson, ten leagues from Puerto Palomas. I sent my secretary, Vicente Aldana, on a mission with twenty men to go to the town to collect the export duty of a herd of cattle that was being transported to the other side. He collected the export duty, which amounted to the sum of ten thousand dollars, and went to the United States. After this bad conduct by my secretary, the few people whom I had left felt even more demoralized. I sent Colonel Manuel Gutiérrez and Lieutenant Colonel Tomás Pérez on a commission to the valley with forty men. With seventeen troops, I set up my headquarters in the sierra.

MÁXIMO CASTILLO IS ALL ALONE

I spent a long time on the defensive. Large groups of Villistas and Carrancistas pursued me, and I had few troops left, so that I could not confront them in battle. Colonel Gutiérrez and Lieutenant Pérez took the valley, and that same day, the enemy attacked and defeated them.

On the 12th, a large group of enemies ambushed me. They wounded one of my comrades, and I lost all of my horses and provisions. My troops survived, scattering into different directions, and six went with me. Once we had recovered from our surprise, we returned and attacked the enemy, which was picking up our camp. We repelled them from our camp. Soon darkness fell, and seeing that it was impossible to retake our camp with only six men, I retreated one or two kilometers from the lines of the enemy. I slept there that night. I made a big fire to see if it was possible to gather all of my seventeen troops so that we could attack the enemy at dawn. But none of my comrades showed up all night.

On February 13, 1914, after walking on foot and without food, I talked with my six comrades and asked them what we should do. We agreed to go to El Paso to see if it was possible to pass over [to the United States] and bring one hundred men who had wanted to leave and join me some time ago and who had not been able to cross over because they were not able to travel to Columbus, where they could cross [the border]. I thought that I could bring these people [across the border line] with the two thousand pesos that I [still] had. We decided to go to El Paso, Texas. We advanced to the border, and on the night of the 16th, after four days of walking, and without a bite to eat, we crossed the U.S.-Mexican border.

MÁXIMO CASTILLO, PRISONER IN THE UNITED STATES

The agreement was to split up so that the North American soldiers would not notice us once we got to the border. We planned to meet at a predetermined place in El Paso where we could arrange our affairs and leave as soon as possible. But because the night was so foggy and dark, we did not see the wire fence of the borderline. When day broke on the 17th, we were all together on the other side of the line. We went to a nearby sierra to hide, but because we did not know the terrain of the sierra, we happened upon a camp of *negros* who had been watching us since our arrival at the border. Because we were enemies of Villa, they detained us and sent us to El Paso as prisoners.[63]

We slept. Just before dawn on February 18, a crowd of North Americans arrived, women and men who were eager to get to know me as the most famous fiend of the world. Some of them were permitted to enter and to get as close as my prison cell. They spoke in their language and withdrew as if they feared that I would devour them with my gaze. I observed this spectacle with sorrow and indignation. "These people see me as the most fearsome fiend of the universe." I spent five days like that, and they did not let me rest even for half an hour. Sometimes they came up to the bars of my prison cell, and sometimes they took me outside to present me to the throng crowding together at the prison entrance. When I faced the crowd, an infinite number of cameras focused on me. This entire process tormented me exceedingly; and in particular, a word I was able to make out among all the others that were uttered: "Castillo bandido." That expression made me extremely angry. I was ashamed and wished I were able to speak English to contradict them. I spoke to them in Spanish:

—Gentlemen, I am not a bandit; I am honorable. My enemies and the enemy press have given me that shameful title, but I am not like that. Get to know me as an honorable person. I am an idealistic revolutionary who seeks the betterment of my beloved fatherland. I have been fighting for four years on the battlefield to obtain benefits for my poor brothers in Mexico. I have fought to make sure that the land, of which there is a copious amount, will be redistributed among the poor peasants; and to ensure that there will be many schools so that our children can receive an education. That is the man-fiend you are contemplating with so much astonishment. I am not a bandit as you have been told.[64]

I spoke in vain; no one understood me. They returned me to my cell. Although it was horrible, I felt better [there] than in the presence of so many agitated people. The whole world had closed in on me.

I buried my head in my hands. My eyes filled with tears. I gave myself to somber meditations about human affairs, and [my] fateful, unjust imprisonment. "Ah, poor wretch of a man," I exclaimed with profound sorrow. I could not resist my tribulations, since I had never before been imprisoned.[65]

RECOGNIZING HUERTA

Taking advantage of my great dejection, General Salazar had the temerity to ask me [once again] to recognize Huerta's government. Because of the reports rendered by all of the revolutionary generals regarding my person, Huerta held me in high regard. Whether in good or bad faith, he told me that he had always fought for our ideals, and that he had recognized the Huerta government with the sole purpose of obtaining the large amount of resources that we needed so that he could later demand of him the fulfillment of the ideals of the revolution. If I was ready to recognize the government, he said, he would immediately send a telegram to Huerta. He was certain that [Huerta] would immediately send plenty of resources to my family and me, and that he would take it upon himself to arrange for my release. I would be free very soon.

Despite the great appreciation I had always had for my general, I could not resist the great offense that his propositions represented. I told him in anger:

—My general, I have children. In spite of my sufferings and their own, I would rather die than to leave them this blot, this indelible stain of treason.

He answered:

—Mr. Castillo, there is no one anymore who fights for a just cause. All of them fight for their own ambition; and we, the stupid ones, sacrifice ourselves for the benefit of these ambitious people.[66]

—That may be so, my general, but it's not possible for me to accept your proposal.

The same day that [Salazar] made these propositions, Sr. Carrascosa came to visit me. He was a friend and comrade who had always worked for our cause. He made the same suggestions that Salazar had put forward. He told me that Huerta was going to dominate the situation, and that we should join him so as not to slip into oblivion. Of course, he said, we would receive assistance from him; our families had many needs, and the agrarian problem was nothing but a farce, as everyone was fighting for their personal gain. He told me that he had a letter for me from Huerta's consul, and that the government would gladly accept my support and that it would do all it could to obtain my freedom; it would also send the funds that I needed for my [legal] defense.

When I heard these words from the people who had been my comrades, my heart sank with sadness and indignation. My mind got all worked up, and I started to meditate about the events of the past, evoking in my mind serious and deep thoughts. I completely rejected the propositions of my former allies; and I refused to receive the letter from the consul that Mr. Carrascosa had brought. I asked him not to mention the murderer and traitor Huerta again. He got upset, but he did not speak of him again.

Thus I spent more than a month of suffering in my odious cell, secured by three keys and a sentry on watch. I had no other consolation except to talk to General Salazar about our work and the adventures of the revolution. I was able to see my wife and my children once every three days when they were allowed to visit me in the prison. To be sure, the visits from my family only increased my agony. When they were with me, their eyes were wet with tears, seeing the strict vigilance to which I was subjected as well as the harsh treatment by the guards. I did not do the same [and kept myself under control] in order not to add to their suffering.

At times, the guard forgot to put both of the locks on the cell door, and they only put one of them—although it made no difference, I felt great relief at [being locked away by] a single key.

That is the way I spent the beginning of my prison term until April 4 in the morning, when we were told that they were going to take us to a camp with the other prisoners. They took us at 4:00 p.m. They already had two tents, each inside a small wire pen of twenty square feet. At that point, General Salazar and I felt very good because we were in fresh air. We saw our compatriots and greeted each other, albeit from far away. I saw my comrades and my brother, Apolonio, and talked to them for a while. They kept them in a pen right next to ours, and one could communicate by raising one's voice just a little. We sat down in the entrances of our tents to watch the high fence and the crowd of Mexican prisoners. Although we were not free, we felt a bit of relief watching the visitors. We read the press and informed ourselves about the events occurring in Mexico. We spent two very nice days.

THE HARASSMENT IN PRISON

By coincidence, I did not notice anything strange during those two days, but on the third day, I observed that the North American soldiers not only treated the prisoners badly, but also the Mexicans who visited us. That day, I saw a Mexican one foot inside the wire fence designed to prevent the [visitors] from moving close to us. The soldiers kicked him until he was on the other side of the wire. When I saw this behavior, I got so angry that I stopped breathing, but there was nothing that I could do.[67]

From that day on, similar things kept happening, and I was sorry to be there [to witness it]; I would have preferred to be in my cell so that I would not have to see the abuses they were committing toward our race. And these things kept getting worse until the events of Tampico and Veracruz.

On April 22, 1914, we observed quite a bit of alarm and movement among the North American soldiers. They kept running from one side to the other and talked a lot, and we did not have any idea what was happening. The only thing I understood was "Castillo . . ." and "Salazar . . ." They put a stop to our visits; at night, they were not allowed to come close and talk to us; we were forbidden to read the press, and they doubled the sentries on watch. Instead of one, they used two of them. When darkness fell, a captain ordered the sentries to kill Salazar and me upon the slightest movement in the camp; there was a rumor that the Mexicans wanted to free us that night. That is what General Salazar understood them to say. He told me, and I replied:

—Well, we will die here like the snakes. In a little while, they will kill us in our sleep. But there is no way out; if it comes to that, we will die, but with bravery . . . We don't have to act intimidated.

I told the general this because I felt my legs slackening and my breath taken away. While we were talking about this in low voices, the soldiers encircled our tents. They all loaded their guns, and a few pointed them at us as if to practice. We were afraid that they would accidentally fire a shot, and that they would kill us and then claim that it was an accident. Finally, I told General Salazar:

—Let's go to bed, so that we don't have to continue to watch the stunts of those poor wretches.

We lay down, but it was no use. I could not sleep a wink. I spent the night awake, listening to the movement and the noise that they were making: loading and unloading their weapons and talking nonstop. For a while, I expected that upon the slightest sign of trouble among the other prisoners or anything that occurred in El Paso, they would kill us immediately. That was my fear, and since I could not chase it away, I sensed that my breathing stopped. "What is happening to me?" I asked myself trying to distract my attention a little, but it was impossible.

It is very sad to die defenseless. But I gathered courage by realizing that death was the same, whether one defended oneself or died defenseless; it was no more than a moment of sacrifice. But it was worse to die with the reputation of a bandit, when I had the satisfaction of knowing that I was the most honorable of all of the revolutionaries. That is how I spent the night until dawn.

On the 23rd, I got up early. I washed my face, which woke me up. I asked General Salazar:

—What's new?

—"Nothing," he answered. "Only what happened last night."

In fact, everything was normal—except that no one visited us anymore, and that they did not let us read the newspapers anymore. We did not know anything while there was great alarm in El Paso. At noon, my wife arrived scared and quivering, and she could hardly say hello to me. I asked her:

—What's new?

She replied:

—The intervention. People are very scared because they say that the Villistas will attack El Paso, and that the North Americans will attack Cd. Juárez. There have been large movements of North American troops.

—Well, my daughter, here the soldiers also scared us last night. By the movements they were making and a few words that we were able to understand, we thought that the situation was grave, and that the general and I were in danger.

She started crying and said:

—You are not doing well here; I will go to the attorney now so that they take you back to the cell, because you will be in less danger there.

—I think so, too. Do what you like, but they can kill us there as well as here if they want.

I wanted to relieve her worries telling her that they were not going to kill us, and if they did, my body would perish, but my memory would exist forever like that of Hidalgo . . . like that of Juárez . . . or like that of a bandit . . .

She interrupted me and said:

—And how is that going to help your children and me if we are not going to see you anymore?

She started to cry even harder and told me between sobs:

—I am leaving; I will see the attorney right now to see what he can do for you.

—Go, then, my beloved wife; divine Providence has got to help us.

My beloved wife left, and I stayed feeling more tormented than ever. She came back in the afternoon:

—I came to bring a letter to the colonel from the lawyer, asking him to take you to the cell. He said yes, within three or four days.

—Go, then, my dear . . . don't wear yourself out anymore.

Night fell on the 23rd. I went to bed early to see if I could sleep. I felt very much unhinged and fell asleep soon thereafter. But it would have been better if I had not been able to sleep, because I received a great shock when I awoke at 11:00 p.m. from the sound of a shout accompanied by a whistle—a kind of buzzer that came in through my senses and crept all the way to my feet and made me tremble. I heard more shouts in rapid succession, and I heard the din of the soldiers, all of whom started to move about and load their weapons. "What is this ruckus all about?" I asked myself.

I uncovered my face and saw darkness. I saw that they had lit a light in the entrance of my tent; then a soldier entered and illuminated my face with a match. He recognized me and left. Then I heard the jumble of someone on horseback who came and left at top speed. Among all the noise they were making, I frequently heard "Castillo . . ." and "Salazar . . ." They encircled the tents and continued to illuminate our tents with matches. But then I noticed the darkness . . . I had not remembered that it was not supposed to be dark because we had had electrical lighting before. "Well, without a doubt, they will shoot us; but if that is so, I will be very content because I slept so well for a little while." Then I heard the noise of a cart that was being brought in. "Well, without a doubt, they will shoot us, and they will take away our corpses in that cart."

Suddenly, the lighting lit up, as bright as daylight. "They have switched on the light to line up the firing squad. I hope they drill ten shots into me at once so that I can die instantly and they don't make me suffer." With the appearance of the light, the din of the soldiers began to subside; my nervousness lessened, and I dozed off and on until dawn, awaiting the impending sad end before us. I got up. I found the general looking very serious and greeted him. I asked him:

—How did you spend the night, my general?

—"Like hell," he answered. "They did not let me sleep after those phonies cut the light off and made an awful uproar; they thought we were fleeing."

Then I remembered that we had had lighting [before I had gone to sleep], and that the outage had occasioned the movements. We calmed ourselves down a bit, as everything appeared quiet. My wife came and told me that everyone was very calm, and that the excitement in the fort had very much died down.

CASTILLO'S RESENTMENTS

We spent three or four days feeling calmer, albeit frustrated that we could not follow the events that unfolded between the United States and Mexico. On April 28, 1914, we received notice that they would take us to a fort in New Mexico and that things were not going well: intervention was inevitable.

My distress returned once again. One day I found out that they were going to take all of us, and that we would leave on May 4. When I heard the news, I found myself immensely confused, and my thoughts were so heavy that I did not know what to do. I was trying to imagine what I could do with my family, or what would happen to them in El Paso without resources . . . "and I will be over there, exiled and imprisoned, without knowing what will happen to them and how they will survive." These thoughts tormented me, and every once in a while, I cursed myself:

—I have been a revolutionary for four years, and I never sought a single peso for my own future because I tried to be too honorable. If I had wanted to, I would have made many thousands of pesos in the revolution, and then I would not have to worry about my family suffering. Now, only God knows how they will live. And to make matters worse, Villa confiscated my small farm in Chihuahua, which helped me earn some income, just because I called him a thief . . . In the end, God is very great and keeps a worm within a rock . . . He will take care of my family.

I spent five days with such thoughts, thoughts that made my heart sink. I pondered our exile, and where they were going to take us, and what they would do with my family: whether I would be able to take them with me so that they could suffer at my side, or whether I would leave them and not know their fate. I did not have any hope that some friend or ally would give them protection, because all of them had abandoned me the moment I was detained. No matter how much I wrote to them from my prison cell, none of them deigned to answer me.

I was very upset with my political allies, from the first to the last. When I was in the revolution, all of them wrote to me; they all praised me, and they all asked me for money for the sacred cause . . . and I gave money to all of them. Once they found out about my imprisonment, none of them even condescended to greet me . . . [A]ll of them had disappeared.

I convinced myself that such is human nature, and that there was not such a thing as friends or allies in a just cause. In particular, all of the politicians are ambitious and support a cause when they see that [the cause can help them] succeed in their personal ambitions. They will flatter the one who sacrifices and risks his life with honesty and good intentions; but if they see that such a person might fail, they will simply toady to the party that presents them with the greatest opportunities, and they will turn their backs to the one whom they had originally supported and who had sacrificed himself for their benefit. That is what happened to me; now that I had been imprisoned because of my own misfortune, all of them disappeared. But if I come out of prison one day and they see that they can obtain by means of my sacrifices one of the high [political] posts that they desire, I am sure that they will all appear and pay homage to me. That is what General Salazar had told me during our meeting in the station of San Pedro. He said that all of those politicians who supported me then would abandon me as soon as they saw me in difficulties, and that they were not fighting for ideals but for their own convenience.

Finally, May 3 arrived, the eve of my departure for my new prison. At 11:00 a.m., my wife and children came to say good-bye. The hour that they were with me seemed to last forever, because the scene we presented was the saddest in my entire life. When I could not stand it anymore, I told them to leave, and they departed, drowned in tears. I returned to my cell to lament my sad situation.

The day of the 4th dawned, and the hour of our departure came. My children shed more tears when they heard the train announcing our departure.

THE NEW PRISON

On May 5, 1914, we awoke in our camp, and they immediately crammed Salazar and me into a new cell, a worse one than the one in Ft. Bliss: dark, cold, and filthy. I wrote to my family right away to let them know of my sad situation. My wife then went to see how she could help me in my suffering. My brother Apolonio's wife accompanied her. They took a train that passes by near the camp.

On May 12, they alit from the train at 11:00 p.m. at a station near the camp. The station house was dark and silent, and they decided not to go there. Because they were afraid of bad people, they decided to stay close to the railroad track. They did not know where the camp was: neither the direction nor the distance. The night was rainy and cold. They spent the night without sleeping a wink, afraid and cold, and worried that the two little children of my brother would get sick. They cried because of the cold. They spent the night not knowing what to do.

By coincidence, when day broke on the 14th, a North American came by with a wagon and took them to the camp. They allowed my wife to speak to me. I was horrified to see her so pale, shivering with cold. They had spent the night in the dampness, and they had not eaten in twenty-four hours. I tried to talk to the commander of the guard to ask for security for her, but it was not possible to get permission to speak with him. I sent my wife to the camp, and she approached my brother's tent. Since I did not know if they had let them enter the camp, I was worried about where they would stay the next night, and if they would stay out in the open again. My suffering redoubled, thinking about the hardship of my beloved wife. Her suffering and her tears tormented me so excessively that I do not know how to describe it.

Finally, Providence had it that at noon on the 16th, when I least expected it, the head of the guard told me:

—Get ready; we are going to the camp.

I left that moment, and once I was in the camp, reunited with my wife and receiving visits from a great number of friends and comrades-in-arms, my sorrow abated. It seemed to me as if I were no longer a prisoner. My only source of sadness was not being able to see my children, who had stayed in El Paso by themselves. I spent four months of my imprisonment like this in the camp, suffering nothing worse than the bad treatment that we always received, and poor nourishment.

They viewed me with a certain degree of displeasure because they believed that I was responsible for what happened in the Cumbre Tunnel. They gave me a worse tent than the others, so small that both the heat and the cold bothered us, and they gave me fewer provisions. But I put up with all of that without saying a word, and least of all to the North Americans—and maybe that is why they treated me more harshly than all of the others. I tried to conduct myself as well as I could and not cause any trouble, but in spite of all that, they viewed me with contempt.

At the end of September, they opened the prison. On the 28th, they began to take down the fence. To keep us secure, they returned three of my comrades and me (Salazar, Colonel Rodrigo Quevedo, and Major

Jesús San Martín) to our prison cells,[68] until the day when we returned to Ft. Bliss, where they once again put us into a small pen that they had already prepared for us. The four of us stayed together. It seemed that they watched us more closely than before. Every time the guard changed, we heard them make special mention of Salazar and myself. They began to cut back on our food; and they gave us the soldiers' left-overs. Finally, they took Salazar to Albuquerque to stand trial for his offense, and there, he was able to escape. After Salazar's departure, they redoubled the vigilance of the three of us, the only remaining prisoners. They began to treat us even worse. Day and night, they came into our tents every half hour, and one could always hear a voice saying ". . . especially Castillo."

So I have been in prison for one year with tremendous suffering and humiliation, without ever hearing a single word about the reason for my imprisonment. Today, February 19, 1915, marks the anniversary of stepping for the first time across the threshold of my prison. I have spent this day in sadness, remembering that I have been [in prison] for one year; and to make matters worse, they played military music close to our tents, where we could hear it perfectly well. They played a few beautiful notes, but it only made me feel worse.

I told my comrades that the music was beautiful for those who are free; but for those of us who are imprisoned, it serves to increase our suffering. When I hear this music, I feel my chest constricting, and it makes me remember the times when I was young and I lived happily and freely among my friends.

These memories make me pass through bitter moments, seeing myself unjustly deprived of my freedom right now, without the slightest hope that I will be able to get out. To the contrary, it seems that they watch us even more. But we should neither give up nor lose hope to obtain our liberty some day; to return to serve our fatherland in some way; and to see our efforts crowned—the triumph of our sacred cause.

THE MEMOIRS REMAIN INCONCLUSIVE

I stayed in prison for one year and fifteen days without any hope whatsoever. At 8:00 p.m. on March 5, 1915, when I lay in bed naked, three individuals came into my tent: one lieutenant, the superior of the soldiers who guarded us, the inspector of immigration, and another who called himself the secretary of the chief of immigration. I was very surprised to see these people close to me. I began to imagine that they would hold me hostage and send me to Juárez so that the Villistas could assassinate me. It made sense that I thought in those terms; only a few days before, they had taken Mr. Jesús Balderrama across the border incognito and let the Villistas execute him by firing squad for the "crime" of having worked for Don Lea's candidacy for mayor of [Cd. Juárez].

When they were already close to me, the inspector of immigration told me that he wanted to talk to me. I sat up, naked, turned on the light and invited them to sit down. Once they were seated, he told me:

—Do you know that I am the inspector of immigration?

—"Yes, sir," I replied.

—Do you swear to tell the truth about what I am about to ask you?

—Yes, sir.

The first question was:

—Do you know why you have been imprisoned here?

—Sir, I do not know more than what they say in the press, which is that they believe that I am responsible for what happened in the Cumbre Tunnel. But neither the government nor any North American authority has told me why they have kept me here.

He answered:

—I know that they have kept you here unjustly, but yes, they do hold you and your men responsible for the events in the tunnel where sixty people died, including a number of North Americans.

He continued to ask many other questions, for example, where I was when the events in the tunnel happened, where my men were, and if I had given the orders to burn the tunnel. Then he asked me what party I belonged to, how old I was, where I was from, if I was married, if I had children, if I worked . . . and many other questions that would be tiresome to repeat. When his investigation was finished, he told me.

—All of the information I have recorded from you is with the purpose of finding out if you will be admitted here in the United States, to see if you can stay here or will be thrown out of the country.

When I heard those words, I was in a state of shock. I thought that they would probably set me free soon, "or maybe, if I am not welcome in the United States, they will throw me out of here . . . but they should not deport me and hand me over unarmed to the Villistas!"

—It's all right. You do not want to see me here; let me go and give me one hour to leave this republic; and I will do so gladly.

On the 25th of the same month, the immigration agent returned to ask me more questions and to clarify the previous ones. The new questions that they asked me were the following:

—If the North American government should wish to deport you to Mexico, where will you go?

—"Where Zapata is," I answered, "but since I can't get there because he is surrounded by his enemies, I don't know where to go. Over there, Carranza and Villa control all of the villages. No matter where I go, I will be in danger."

—"In that case, if we do not deport you to Mexico because your life is at risk no matter where you go, you will need to stay here under the custody of North American soldiers until peace has returned, along with a government that guarantees [your safety]," he said. He continued: "You have been detained here because you entered this republic at a place that was not a point of entry. You should have entered through a point of entry and gone to the immigration office."

—Very well, sir, so I am not in prison for the reason that you gave me before . . . for the events in the Cumbre Tunnel?

—No, you are in prison because you did not present yourself to the immigration office.

He left, and I continued in despair. I passed more time imprisoned, completely abandoned by my allies and friends. The honorable and brave Major Domitilo Valenzuela was the only one who visited me. He did everything in his power to put me in touch with General Zapata. Since I knew that there had been Zapatista delegates at the Convention of Aguascalientes, and among them, don Paulino Martínez, I immediately . . .[69]

THE DÉNOUEMENT

JESÚS VARGAS VALDÉS

THE END

The memoirs of General Máximo Castillo conclude at the end of 1915, when an immigration inspector came to his cell to inform him that the government of the United States had decided that he was not guilty of the explosion of the train and that they would set him free. However, the inspector continued, in light of the fact that he was not safe in Mexico and his life was in danger, he would need to remain in the custody of North American soldiers until peace returned to Mexico as well as a government that would give him guarantees. We do not know what happened after that, because the last pages of the memoirs went astray in the course of eighty long years.

We know that he remained a prisoner on U.S. territory as late as December 11, 1915, because the newspaper *La Patria* reported that day that [Castillo] was asking for his deportation to Mexico under the condition that they send him to territory dominated by the Zapatista forces. The notice ended as follows: ". . . Castillo is believed to be responsible for the explosion of the Cumbre Tunnel along with another individual by the name of Jesús San Martín. For that reason, it is very likely that these 'Vazquistas' will remain in prison indefinitely until it is possible to send them to Mexico."

It is possible that [Castillo] was released and sent to Cuba during the year 1916; however, among the documents in the family archive is a postcard from his granddaughter, Natividad Vargas Castillo, with the following message: "I dedicate this humble souvenir to my beloved grandparents, as evidence of the friendship and affection of their little niece, Natividad Vargas, one year old." The postcard was sent from Chihuahua to El Paso on December 25, 1917, and we can infer from the content of the message that the grandparents of the little girl, don Máximo and doña Jesusita, were still [in El Paso].

Several months before that date (or perhaps years), doña Jesusita Flores had decided to move to El Paso to be close to her husband and to find a way to help him. Their two children were already old enough to work, and they surely took charge of the sustenance [of the family]. In February 1914, at almost the same time that the general had been arrested in U.S. territory, the Villista government of the state of Chihuahua had declared [Castillo] an enemy of the revolution, and it had decreed the confiscation of his small house in the Santo Niño neighborhood. Under those conditions, doña Jesusita continued to wait while the general remained in the custody of the U.S. Army, most likely until the end of 1917.

We do not know the reason why he was deported to Havana, Cuba, but one might surmise that the government of the United States resolved to do so because it believed that his life was in danger if it set him free in Mexican territory. Don Máximo Vargas told us that he had heard that his grandmother, doña Jesusita, had traveled to Havana to visit her husband. She had found him in deplorable conditions, surviving by peddling vegetables in the streets, pulling a rickety cart. The general could pull the cart only with great difficulty because he suffered from severe arthritis as a consequence of the many years of working in the mines and other occupations in which his body was exposed to the cold as well as humidity.

The general spent the last years of his life far away from his fatherland, the victim of the unjust verdict imposed by the gruesomeness of a political landscape that he had not been able to interpret. He was maltreated by all of the factions, forgotten by his friends, and completely ignored by the Carrancistas who had taken over the government as well as the glory of a civil war that had begun for an ideal and ended in a new dictatorship in disguise.

One sad day in 1919—a distant day that did not merit being recorded in history—[Castillo] died in silence, a part of history but unremembered, which is what happened to almost all of the true revolutionaries.

That same year also brought the passing of Generals Felipe Angeles and Emiliano Zapata, two other great dreamers and idealists of the Mexican Revolution. [Castillo] was a man who thought of others, who sacrificed the love of his children and his wife, the affections and roots of his homeland, and even his own person because he had ideals and because he believed that the poor had a right to a better life.[1]

TIMELINE*

1864	March 11: Máximo Castillo's birth in San Nicolás de Carretas
1881	Marriage with María de Jesús Flores
1896	Elected *presidente municipal* of his hometown but refuses to serve because he does not want to form part of the Porfirian bureaucracy
1898	Begins work in the Cusihuiriáchic mine
1907	Works in the United States
1908	First contact with Mexican revolutionaries
1910	November 9: Commits to participating in the planned uprising November 20: Beginning of Mexican Revolution in response to Francisco I. Madero's Plan of San Luis Potosí
1911	March 6: Participates in failed attack on Casas Grandes, where he saves Madero's life May 10: Participates in the seizure of Ciudad Juárez from government forces
1912	February: Breaks with Madero's government March 7: Promoted to lieutenant colonel by General Pascual Orozco; participates in Orozquista Rebellion
1913	February: Coup d'état of General Victoriano Huerta ends Madero's government and life; Orozco allies with Huerta; Castillo breaks with Orozco. March: Fights under the Zapatista banner as an independent revolutionary

* Adapted from Jesús Vargas Valdés, ed., *Máximo Castillo y la revolución en Chihuahua* (Chihuahua City: Biblioteca Chihuahuense, 2009), 313–16.

1913	May: Carries out land reform on six haciendas
	December: Targeted by attacks by Pancho Villa's forces
1914	February: Defeated by Pancho Villa's forces
	February 16: Crosses border into El Paso
	February 17: Arrested by U.S. border guards; detained at Fort Bliss; writes memoirs
	May 4: Sent to Fort Wingate, New Mexico
1916	Sent to Havana, Cuba (date unknown)
1919	Dies in Havana (date unknown)

NOTES FROM THE EDITOR

INTRODUCTORY MATERIAL

1. Nonetheless, much remains to be done. There are documentary collections and archives that have not received systematic attention, as well as library collections and testimonials of protagonists [of the revolution] that have not yet appeared and continue to wait for their encounter with historiography.

2. In May 1991, Editores Meridiano 107 published an abbreviated version of this testimonial prepared by Jesús Vargas with the title *Máximo Castillo: El zapatista del norte*. Since then, several newspaper and magazine articles have cited this document, but this is the complete version released for the first time.

3. Francisco R. Almada, *Diccionario de historia, geografía y biografía chihuahuenses* (Chihuahua City: Centro Librero La Prensa), 96.

4. Florence C. and Robert H. Lister, *Chihuahua: Almacén de tempestades*, 3rd Spanish ed. (Chihuahua City: Gobierno del Estado de Chihuahua, 1992), 268–69.

5. Francisco Ontiveros, *Toribio Ortega y la Brigada González Ortega* (Chihuahua, 1914), 69. With a print run of only several copies, this book constitutes a very important testimonial for the study of the development of the revolution in the region of Ojinaga from 1910 to the moment of General Toribio Ortega's death. Recently, after almost ninety years, the secretaría de educación y cultura of the state of Chihuahua has prepared a new edition of this text.

6. Benjamín Herrera Vargas, "Breve historia de Máximo Castillo," in *Aquí Chihuahua! Cuna y chispa de la revolución mexicana*, n.p., n.d., 562.

7. The Partido Liberal Mexicano emerged as an organization with a democratic structure. At the aforementioned congress, [the Liberals] defined the following objectives: (1) the respect and exact observance of the laws; (2) the liberal and civic education of the nation; (3) the reestablishment of the political honesty of the public servants; (4) the abolition of any personalist tendency in the government that might countervail the Constitution of 1857 and the Laws of Reform.

8. Heliodoro Olea was born in the village of Bachíniva in 1863. At forty years of age, he stood for election as mayor of that small town, with the support of most of the citizens. In January 1904, he took office. But, as was common in those years, the caciques conspired

against him, and in December of that same year, they removed him from office with the help of interim governor Enrique Creel. In his place, they imposed Pablo Baray.

Olea sent a letter to Ricardo Flores Magón denouncing the illegal nature of these proceedings, and in response, he received the following advice: "If the people do not resolve en masse to throw off this yoke, we will continue to suffer the most terrible vexations of the ruling caciques, from the monarch to the local bully . . ." From this moment on, Olea became interested in Magonismo and remained in constant contact with the editors of the newspaper *Regeneración.*

On November 14, 1906, he was arrested and imprisoned in Cd. Guerrero. Later on, [the authorities] sent him to the Chihuahua penitentiary, and finally to San Juan Ulúa, where he met Juan Sarabia and other Magonistas imprisoned there. After participating in the revolution against Porfirio Díaz, he wrote down his revolutionary experiences and died on June 25, 1945.

9. Official correspondence of Secretario de Relaciones Exteriores Enrique C. Creel, private collection of Jesús Vargas (photocopies).

10. It is useful to remember that in 1910, elections did not take place via direct popular vote of all citizens. The prevailing system featured a decision via so-called electoral councils that included several citizens who had been elected to that end. The direct vote for the election of deputies, senators, and the president of the republic was used for the first time on April 26, 1912, precisely during the government of President Madero.

11. Official correspondence of Secretario de Relaciones Exteriores Enrique C. Creel.

12. Ibid.

13. Ibid.

14. Juan Gualberto Amaya, *Madero y los auténticos revolucionarios de 1910,* 1st ed. (Mexico City, 1946), 104.

15. Roque Estrada, *La revolución y Francisco I. Madero,* facs. ed. (Mexico City: Instituto Nacional de Estudios Históricos de la Revolución Mexicana, 1985), 167.

16. Interview, Jesús Vargas with Mr. Antonio Orozco at his house in Chihuahua City, March 6, 1996.

17. Regarding this issue, see Estrada, *La revolución y Francisco I. Madero,* 168: Parral. The anti-reelectionist cause was stronger here than in Chihuahua itself and involved all social classes. Its leaders were the most renowned capitalists, such as the Bacas, much appreciated by the people. This new circumstance confirms my observation above regarding anti-reelectionism in the state of Chihuahua. It not only indicates the [widespread] conviction about its necessity, but it also involved the hope of its easiest development since its leadership included skillful people with some monetary means.

18. See the complete text of the Plan de la Empacadora and the document signed that day in the appendix to the original Spanish version of the book.

19. Mr. Daniel Fourzán, a neighbor of Máximo Castillo in the Colonia Santo Niño, told us in an interview dated December 18, 1988, the following story. In 1910, when he was ten years old, he was an eyewitness to a meeting of revolutionaries in don Máximo's forge, with the purpose of preparing the uprising of November 20. He also provided that same information during a ceremony held to memorialize the death of don Abraham González.

20. In the *Revista Chihuahuense* dated November 15, 1911, José María Ponce de León published the following important document that surveys the principal activities in which the authors, Cástulo Herrera and Antonio Ruiz, participated from November 1910 to May 1911. According to this document, twelve people met at Máximo Castillo's house on November 2, 1910, at 10:00 a.m., for the purpose of planning the seizure of the Chihuahua City fortifications. See volume 2 of the collection of that journal in the Sala Chihuahua of the CIDECH.

21. It must be noted that accordingly, the ranch house of the Hacienda San Diego, a property of the Terrazas clan, was the first National Palace of the revolutionary government.

22. Francisco R. Almada, *La revolución en el estado de Chihuahua* (Mexico City: Instituto Nacional de Estudios Históricos de la Revolución Mexicana, 1964), 1:201.

23. See the reference made by Francisco I. Madero with respect to the fact that he had not acceded to Orozco's and Villa's pretensions on that occasion, in the sense of changing the makeup of his revolutionary cabinet. In Comisión de Investigaciones Históricas de la Revolución Mexicana, *Documentos históricos de la revolución mexicana,* series "Revolución y régimen maderista" (Mexico City: JUS, 1965), 2:35.

24. Marcelo Caraveo, *Crónica de la revolución (1910–1929)* (Mexico City: Trillas, 1991), 52.

25. *Documentos históricos de la revolución mexicana* (serie "Revolución y régimen maderista," 2:92–132) transcribes the work of this convention.

26. Gobierno del Estado de Chihuahua, *La revolución de Chihuahua en las páginas del periódico El Padre Padilla,* vol. 2, 1st ed., 2001, 587.

27. Comisión de Investigaciones Históricas de la Revolución Mexicana, *Documentos históricos de la revolución mexicana,* 341–42. [Translator's note: This document has been translated numerous times; the English text comes from John Womack, *Emiliano Zapata and the Mexican Revolution* (New York: Knopf, 1969), 400–402.]

28. Gobierno del Estado de Chihuahua, *La revolución de Chihuahua,* 665.

29. Amaya, op. cit., 362.

30. Michael C. Meyer, *El rebelde del norte: Pascual Orozco y la revolución* (Mexico City: UNAM, 1984), 92.

31. Alfonso Taracena, *Madero,* 581–83, cited in Amaya, op. cit., 404.

32. Almada, *La revolución en el estado de Chihuahua,* 2:21–22.

33. Nomination signed by Emilio Vázquez Gómez, provisional president of the revolution, March 15, 1913, Palomas, Chihuahua. [Translator's note: This source was supposed to be in the appendix of the original Spanish-language work, but it is not.]

34. With the purpose of correcting those who affirm that Lucio Blanco had put in place the first revolutionary agrarian redistribution in the ranch of Los Borregos in the state of Tamaulipas, the renowned student of agrarismo Andrés Molina Enríquez wrote a clarification in the Mexico City newspaper *Novedades.* In the column "Tribuna Nacional," he indicated that Emiliano Zapata himself had carried out the first agrarian reform on April 30, 1912, in Ixcamilpa de Guerrero in the state of Puebla.

Later in that same clarification, [Molina Enríquez] pointed out that Máximo Castillo ordered the second instance of agrarian reform when he and his people separated from the forces of General José Inés Salazar, who followed Orozco into oblivion. He wrote that

General Máximo Castillo initiated in Chihuahua the subdivision of Terrazas's vast land-holdings—the largest in all of Mexico—by distributing among campesinos the lands of the Hacienda San Luis. This reform then extended to the haciendas San Diego, San Lorenzo, El Carmen, etc. This information was published in the newspaper *Novedades* in Mexico City. We do not have the date of the article, but it is almost certain that it was published between 1938 and 1939.

35. One must also consider the fact that Zapatismo did not grow in Chihuahua because its origin and objectives corresponded to the agrarian problem in the state of Morelos. The history of the agrarian problem in Chihuahua and the expectations of the campesinos were very different and did not find their expression in the Plan of Ayala.

36. *El Liberal, periódico independiente de la mañana*, 2a época, vol. 2, no. 12, August 12, 1913.

37. We do not have information about the location of the original of this document. We only have a photocopy, where the seal of the Mexican Embassy appears, as well as the number 1947 and the date of October 1, 1913.

38. Almada, *La revolución en el estado de Chihuahua*, vol. 2, 43.

39. *El Paso Morning Times*, February 19, 1914.

40. Ibid., February 20, 1914.

41. Ibid.

42. On April 1, 1922, the newspaper *La Patria* published an article about the explosion of the train in the Cumbre Tunnel. Eight years after the event, it reported:

> The rebel chief Manuel Gutiérrez had risen up in arms against the government, after having accepted an amnesty from the new government through the offices of General Rodrigo Quevedo, the chief of provisions of Casas Grandes. Gutiérrez is in Pearson today. He is neither in Mexico City nor in Chihuahua City as has been said.
>
> Gutiérrez is guilty of the explosion of the Cumbre Tunnel, which had been originally imputed to General Máximo Castillo . . .

43. We have not been able to establish the name or the office that this [inspector] occupied in the United States immigration service, because the only reference is the one that Castillo makes in his memoirs.

THE SIMPLE HISTORY OF MY LIFE

1. Since 1686, the town had been known as Puesto de Carretas; thereafter, its name changed to San Nicolás de Carretas. It kept that name until 1933, when it was renamed Gran Morelos, its name up to this day. It is located between Cuauhtémoc and Cusi-huiriáchic. At the beginning of the twentieth century, the town had a population of approximately four thousand inhabitants, all of them mestizos.

2. The name of Castillo's wife was María de Jesús Flores, probably a native of the same village of San Nicolás de Carretas.

3. Despite his poverty and economic difficulties, Máximo Castillo was a campesino who was able to cultivate a plot of land as well as venture into commerce, who could read and write, and who was able to help other people who were even poorer than he was. He

observes the injustice from the outside, since government forces have not bothered him. According to the description of his youth, one can identify him as a midlevel campesino, with leadership qualities that would become apparent at the end of the nineteenth century, when he had turned thirty years old.

4. At the beginning of the twentieth century, the *municipio* of Cusihuiriáchic had 7,400 inhabitants and two silver mines.

5. In those years, the above-mentioned practices in the registration of mining properties were unfortunately commonplace, the result of the efforts of U.S. investors to buy high-quality mines only to engage in speculative sales to the great mining companies. That was the situation Máximo Castillo confronted in the issue of his mine, which he could not sell because of the disagreements between him and his partner. The January 20, 1900, issue of the Chihuahua City newspaper *Idea Libre* published a legal notice of one Matilde Meraz, identifying him as the primary partner of Máximo Castillo and protesting against any purchase contract involving the La Soledad mine.

6. The years following 1890 witnessed an intense influx of migratory Mexican workers who turned to the North American agricultural companies in order to sell their labor. These laborers had no difficulties traveling to [the United States] or acquiring permanent residency. This migration grew to alarming proportions, and the revolutionary organizations blamed the dictatorship [of Porfirio Díaz] for having contributed to the seizure of the [agricultural] property [of these Mexican workers]. The Partido Liberal Mexicano addressed this problem in Article 35 of its 1906 program, where it stated: "The government will repatriate the Mexicans resident abroad who so desire, paying them the cost of their journey and providing them with land for cultivation. Omar Cortés, *El programa del Partido Liberal y sus antecedents* (Mexico City: Antorcha, 1985), [n.p.].

7. On October 19, 1906, the government apprehended Magonista leader Juan Sarabia and several other Chihuahuense revolutionaries implicated in a national insurrection planned for those days. The prisoners were sent to San Juan Ulúa, while Governor [Enrique C.] Creel launched a campaign of repression against all elements in which any Magonista sympathies could be detected. Over the next few years, the majority of the prisoners were released, and some of them joined the revolutionary movement of Pascual Orozco. Among others, one might cite José Porras A., César Canales, Prisciliano Silva, Eduardo González, and Heliodoro Olea. Francisco Almada, *La revolución en el estado de Chihuahua,* 1:112–3 [no publisher given]; and Heliodoro Olea, *Apuntes históricos de la revolución de 1910–1911, de Bachiniva a Ciudad Juárez,* 1st ed. (Chihuahua City: Alffer, 1961), 11–26.

8. Máximo Castillo's house in Chihuahua City is located in a neighborhood where many railroad workers lived, just a few steps from a canteen very much frequented by these workers. The façade of this house still exists in the street named J. Eligio Muñoz number 3108, in the *colonia* Santo Niño.

9. In an article published by *El Heraldo de Chihuahua* on March 8, 1938, Mr. Daniel Fourzán—friend and neighbor of the Castillo family—related the following:

In the kaleidoscope of my nostalgia, the valiant and brave personality of don Abraham González looms large, slipping through the shadows of the night, crossing through my neighborhood with firm steps and hardened spirit until he reached a modest little house. There, he anxiously awaited the arrival of that group of pro-revolutionaries among whom the owner of the house, don Máximo Castillo, distinguished himself, as did his brother, Apolonio, as well as Cástulo Herrera, Maximino González, Felipe Estrada, Cosme Delgado, my father, Nazario Fourzán, and a few others that my unfaithful memory cannot recall . . .

10. In addition to this, Tomás F. Serrano transcribes a memorandum signed by Cástulo Herrera, Seferino Pérez, and Antonio Ruiz that begins with the following paragraph:

On November 10, 1910, at 10:00 p.m., twelve men met at the house of Máximo Castillo with the goal of coordinating the operations to take over the fortress (*plaza*) of Chihuahua. After two hours of discussions, it was decided that the following acts would happen simultaneously at 2:00 am on November 20: dynamite the barracks of the Twelfth and Third Regiments, whose troops had already agreed to disband; to suspend telegraph and telephone service; to turn off electric lighting; to apprehend the principal authorities; and to enter the city with the armed forces that we would have gathered beforehand. It was also decided to name Mr. Pascual Alvarez Tostado chief of operations in the interior of the city. Alvarez Tostado accepted this nomination. See Serrano, *Episodios de la revolución* (El Paso, TX, 1911), 184.

11. Máximo Castillo was a formal man who respected the word he had given. But above all else, he was a revolutionary with well-defined ideals. He opted for the revolution against the wishes of his family because he was convinced that the Porfirian regime was responsible for the poverty in which the majority of Mexicans lived. It seems significant to us that he joined the revolution even though personally, Castillo did not consider himself a victim of the dictatorship. As he himself pointed out, he had prevailed whenever he appealed to the protection of the law. It is also noteworthy that he does not register any objections to the rich clans of Chihuahua represented by the Terrazas-Creel family.

12. Braulio Hernández and Abraham González were the precursors of the revolution in Chihuahua. The conditions that Guadalupe Balderrama describes were symptomatic for the distrust that the common people expressed with respect to the seriousness and determination of intellectuals such as those two. Abraham González and Braulio Hernández, a merchant and a professor, had had little contact with rancheros, and they did not know how to use weapons or horses. Nonetheless, the two men were the primary organizers of the Maderista revolution in Chihuahua.

13. The revolutionary group of Máximo Castillo included a few railroad workers recruited by Cástulo Herrera, who had distinguished himself as the leader of the Boilermakers' Union. During this first phase, Herrera appears as one of Abraham González's closest associates, and all of his comrades, including Francisco Villa, recognized him as their chief.

14. Castillo's reaction reveals with all clarity what middle-class rancheros thought about the bandit Francisco Villa. Some authors, such as Juan Gualberto Amaya (op. cit., 369–70), have referred to sentiments such as these, as seen in documents and testimonials,

as proof that they rejected Villa because of his past. Our suggestion is that the version of the story about the hacendado who wanted to rape Villa's sister—the version that Villa himself told Manuel Bauche Alcalde—was an invention intended to justify his career as a bandit as a consequence of an act of defending the honor of his family. We have not found any documentary evidence that substantiates an attack by Doroteo Arango [Villa's real name] against a hacendado by the name López Negrete.

15. A dispatch by the captain Manuel Sánchez P. relates the following: ". . . barricaded in the railroad station, nearby houses and the mounds of firewood stacked on both sides of the track, a gang of revolutionaries attacked a convoy. The gunfire only lasted for twenty minutes . . . The effect of surprise was considerable, and Col. Yepes perished along with three other soldiers, while eight other soldiers suffered serious injuries." Captain Sánchez notes in his dispatch that "the conductor and machinist stopped the train even though they were ordered repeatedly to continue moving. The train remained stopped during the gunfire and only left when the insurgents began their retreat to the mountains." See the Secretaría de Guerra y Marina's general study of the campaigns that took place from November 18, 1910, to May 25, 1911 (Mexico City: Talleres del Departamento del Estado Mayor, 1913).

16. Heliodoro Olea (op. cit., 34–39) relates that Pascual Orozco encountered the forces of Herrera and Villa, who commanded approximately eighty men, in La Junta on December 10 at 2:00 p.m., and that Orozco proposed that they join his army. According to this version, Orozco and Herrera agreed to coordinate the upcoming battles against the Porfirian army. We know that Orozco sent a message that same evening. The following day, the forces of Herrera and Villa were not present during the fighting at Cerro Prieto. According to Olea, Orozco's mail arrived at the meeting site, and there they informed him that Herrera and eighty other men had split from Francisco Villa and marched toward the United States.

17. After Cástulo Herrera did not follow Orozco's order, Luis A. García let it be known that Villa had cut ties with Herrera and that the latter was marching toward the United States with a group of eighty men. According to Heliodoro Olea (op. cit., 39), "Luis A. García had found out from Sotero Corral—an individual who had followed Herrera and Zeferino [sic] Pérez earlier on—that the intention of these individuals was to go to the United States. Therefore, he sent a message with Encarnación Enríquez, Julio Corral's second-in-command, to Dolores Palomino, Salvador Meza, and Guadalupe Gardea, chiefs who accompanied the aforementioned Herrera. With reference to the good friendship that Enríquez wished to express, his message instructed the recipients to render their assistance to Herrera and Pérez as good Mexicans in case they wanted to go to the United States . . .

Under these circumstances, one can understand Orozco's position vis-à-vis Herrera, and that of Castillo as well. Palomino, Gardea, and Meza returned and joined Orozco's army on December 20 along with the majority of their troops. Castillo could not abandon Herrera and accompanied him to Cd. Juárez, where the two men met with Abraham González. After four weeks, he returned to Orozco, and he was cordially received because he brought a good shipment of ammunition sent by Abraham González.

18. It is clear that by December 1910, the revolutionary forces were split into two factions. One completely accepted the authority of Abraham González and acted under his direct and permanent guidance. Both Cástulo Herrera and Máximo Castillo belonged

to that group. Orozco represented the other faction, which recognized González's overall leadership but maneuvered with ample independence of movement and made its own decisions. From that point on, one could appreciate what would later become the conflict between Orozquistas and Maderistas.

19. Abraham González used different means of communication with the revolutionary groups that concentrated in the area of Cd. Juárez. The version related by Heliodoro Olea (op. cit., 49) complements that of Máximo Castillo. According to his notes, Castillo received the order to advance toward Juárez on January 16, 1911, just like other chiefs such as Luis A. García.

20. The "Esmelta" was the foundry of American Smelting located in El Paso, Texas; Máximo Castillo used it on various occasions as a point of reference.

21. The encounter with Madero's General Staff shows that the mobilization of Cd. Juárez was intended to protect Madero's entry, but it also shows that Pascual Orozco did not recognize the presence of a "General Staff," made up of people who came from outside, without weapons or horses, and without experience in the type of warfare that his men had been waging in the area for the past four months.

22. On November 15, 1910, the leadership of the Partido Liberal Mexicano published a manifesto in which it instructed the party's followers that they should take advantage of Francisco I. Madero's personal interests. In this manner, many Magonistas joined the revolution.

On February 11, 1911, a contingent under the leadership of Prisciliano Silva, a Magonista, took control of the village of Guadalupe and provided protection to Madero so that he could cross the international border. Nonetheless, at his first opportunity, Madero ordered Silva disarmed and apprehended because he had refused to recognize him as provisional president.

The recognition of Madero divided the ranks of the Magonistas. Lázaro Gutiérrez de Lara, who represented the socialist wing, also met with Madero and his staff during that time, and he awarded him his recognition as provisional president and offered him his support.

23. At the same time that Madero attacked Casas Grandes on March 6, 1911, Orozco's forces were in San Isidro, where they received a message [from Madero] that morning. Therefore, it was not possible for Orozco to participate in the attack along with Madero. In the afternoon, Orozco's army got to Galeana, where they received notice of the disaster. It seems incomprehensible that Madero and his council of high command did not give due notice of the decision to attack Casas Grandes. According to some authors, such as Juan Gualberto Amaya (op. cit., 134–35), Madero thought that a victory in Casas Grandes could be easily obtained, and that such a victory would elevate his moral authority over the revolutionary chiefs in Chihuahua and the other parts of the national territory where rebel armies had risen up in revolt.

24. Olea (op. cit., 75) relates this incident as follows: ". . . we found Mr. Madero, who came on foot with a wounded arm. His escort of honor accompanied him; and the bullets that the enemy sent their way were so numerous that in the act of saluting Mr. Madero, they killed Salomón Dozal, the chief of arms of Rayón, who walked on my left. Struck in the forehead, he fell dead to our feet like a bolt of lightning . . ."

25. Col. Samuel García Cuellar, one of the Federal chiefs who participated in the fighting at Casas Grandes, rendered an official dispatch on March 10, 1911. After researching the confrontation in detail, he informed his superiors as follows:

> ... The rebels were headed by Francisco I. Madero, and their number was 700 or 800 ... On the battlefield, we found 58 dead rebels, among them an American citizen by the name of Alberto L. Harrington, who headed up a group of filibusters, as well as two *cabecillas* (minor chiefs): Francisco J. Esteves and José Dolores Palomino; 101 carbines of different systems and calibers, one sword, two machetes; 1,396 cartridges and 60 grenades. We took 41 prisoners, of whom 10 are injured. Among the prisoners are Eduardo F. Hay, who calls himself chief of the General Staff of the Army of Liberation, and a *cabecilla* named Candelario Romero ... Among the dead were five North Americans, and the prisoners include 16 foreigners.

See Secretaría de Guerra y Marina, *Estudio general de las operaciones que han tenido lugar del 18 de noviembre de 1910 al 25 de mayo de 1911, en la parte que corresponde a la Segunda Zona Militar* (Mexico City: Talleres del Departamento de Estado Mayor, 1913).

26. General Marcelo Caraveo relates the following:

> Madero's men had dispersed completely, and he retreated to the village of Galeana, where we had just arrived from San Isidro. To receive Madero, we formed an entourage consisting of Pascual [Orozco], Agustín Estrada, and myself. Madero was short in stature, with a shrieking voice and gawky demeanor, and he was still nervous from the fighting ... In that same place, under the arcades of the town hall, and in the presence of our entire contingent, Madero explained to us the program of the revolution, all in clear and simple words ...

It was in the hacienda of Bustillos where Francisco Villa appeared again, having been pardoned by Madero for all of his antisocial history.

27. At the end of March, there was a serious problem with approximately twenty-five revolutionaries from Namiquipa, who had a disagreement with Abraham González because he had deposed the mayor whom they had elected. The matter got more complicated, and Madero himself needed to intervene and imprison two Namiquipa chiefs, José María Espinoza and Rómulo Rodríguez, who were subjected to a court-martial. Although he does not mention this fact in his memoirs, Máximo Castillo participated in this court-martial. The incident demonstrated the inability of the revolutionary leadership to resolve this kind of problem, where the people made a decision that the chiefs would not accept.

More complicated still was the matter of the socialists who were disarmed and imprisoned for insubordination. Once again, Olea (op. cit., 86–90) contributes much information. He relates that on April 13, in Casas Grandes, Lázaro Alanís gave a speech regarding the Socialist Party. All those who followed this party wore a red emblem. Madero spoke later on, and at the end of the event, those in attendance cheered Madero, Orozco, García, and the Socialist Party. On the 14th, Madero criticized García severely because he had been named the supplier of the army and had not correctly carried out the orders that he had received. Along with this one, there were other reprimands of the Socialists' chiefs. Thus, on the 16th, Lázaro Alanís, Luis A. García, José Parra, Inés Salazar, Leónides Zapata, and Tomás Laza sent a message in which they asked for their separation from the military. Subsequently, Villa's forces apprehended these chiefs, and Villa angrily charged Luis A. García with a pistol in his hand, accusing him of treason. In his work, Olea presents three documents exchanged between the rebels and Madero. This all happened in the station of Guzmán, and on the 18th, the prisoners were sent to Ciudad Guerrero, from where they escaped soon thereafter.

28. Olea (op. cit., 93) presents the following version of this incident: "The night of the 7th, when most in the camp were already asleep, Raúl Madero went from camp to camp on horseback, giving notice of the supposed triumph of the revolution following the telegram announcing the resignation of General Díaz. That telegram was apocryphal; when don Porfirio found out, he ordered General Luque, who was in Ojinaga with five or eight hundred men, to proceed to Juárez to come to Navarro's assistance."

29. Marcelo Caraveo (op. cit., 52) relates the following:

The first confrontation between us, the revolutionaries, and the Madero cabinet occurred when we had collected all of the arms and gear of the Federales. Garibaldi and Roque González wanted us to deliver these armaments to them, and Pascual refused to give them to him, since it was useless in the hands of those who had not fought.

The second confrontation happened when the crowd wanted to shoot Navarro, shouting "Death to the murderer of Cerro Prieto."

The second conflict with Madero occurred because he did not attend to the just petitions of all of us to pay the troops, who went several days without the most elementary means of subsistence . . . Every time that Pascual went to ask for this pay, Madero said he was busy. His daily tasks consisted of interviews with the North American press and celebrating his victory at banquets . . .

30. Olea (op. cit., 103–4) was also an eyewitness of this incident and described it as follows:

The next day, May 12, we went into formation at the door of the anteroom of the headquarters, as we had been ordered to do . . . When we were in formation, Máximo Castillo, the head of President Madero's escort of honor, came out of the anteroom. He told me: "Why this formation, comrade?" I answered him: "It is on the orders of General Orozco . . ."

Heated debates began within the room where the peace should have been discussed; among other things, such as Navarro's execution, Orozco began to accuse Madero of concentrating on the peace treaties and ignoring the people who needed food and provisions . . . And then the [nasty] comments began among the people, to such an extent that someone pushed Abraham González so hard that he crashed against the wall. Those of us who were outside heard an alarming murmuring, and we gave orders to our troops to ready their guns. Villa's men shouted: "Long live Pascual Orozco!" And ours: "Long live President Madero." After a while, President

Madero and his brother, Raúl, came out of the room . . . and got into the automobile . . . Then Orozco came out with his squad pistol in his hand . . . Mr. Madero told him: "But Mr. Orozco, why have you decided to commit this scandalous attack at the most sacred moment for our fatherland; a moment when we are trying to arrange peace?" ". . . Shake this hand as a sign of agreement; let's act as if this was a bad dream. . . ." [Orozco] did not want to shake his hand; José Orozco and I made him do so.

31. This incident showed that neither Orozco nor Villa trusted Madero to a sufficient extent; they considered him incapable of fulfilling his revolutionary goals.

Roque Estrada wrote that he was in the restaurant of the Hotel Sheldon, in El Paso, Texas, between May 17 and 20, 1911. There, he met with Pascual Orozco and Francisco Villa. At the beginning of the conversation, Orozco said the following:

"Does it not seem to you, *Licenciado*, that our president is neither fish nor fowl?" I immediately began the objective and the serious nature of our conference. In light of my desire to restrain them as well as my resolve not to displease them, I just smiled. Orozco and Villa made harsh remarks about Mr. Madero and what they called his cabinet. They concluded by suggesting that I serve as their chief and that the three of us withdraw recognition from Mr. Madero who, in their opinion, could only count on the support of Colonel José de la Luz Blanco . . . Therefore, the embrace between Madero and Orozco after the attempted coup d'état and Villa's forgiveness did not produce a harmonious and benevolent reaction.

See Roque Estrada, *Los señores presidentes, ensamblas históricas* (Mexico City: Chapultepec, 1976), 46.

32. Only a few weeks had gone by since the revolution had triumphed against the dictator Díaz, and the policies of the new government revealed a stark disconnect from the experience of the popular armies during the short period of armed revolutionary conflict. It was no longer up to the people to resolve the problems or decide how they should be resolved; now, it was up to the new government. The old revolutionary fighters would receive a payment as employees of the state, and this payment was certainly very low. However, this passage reflects the fact that there were no more ideals to pursue, because the new government was in charge of making things happen. The principal chiefs of this new government were leaders who did not identify with ordinary people, and who therefore did not represent them.

33. Castillo accepts the commission from a different perspective from that of his comrades. With a small group consisting of sixteen men, he assumes the position of representative of the revolutionary government to help the villagers find justice. In this role, he shows a clear determination to make sure that the election of local representatives reflected the decision of the majority of the population of each village. In contrast, and in accordance with Castillo's version of the events, one can see that General José de la Luz Soto and Francisco Villa understand democracy in a different way, using their military power to impose the candidates of their choice as representatives of each village.

34. One of the things that most displeased the Chihuahuenses was the manipulation of the elections for governor, where Abraham González's personality foreclosed the opportunities for General Pascual Orozco. In the political circles, it was known that González was going to Mexico to occupy a secretariat in November when Madero would assume the presidency of the republic, and thus it happened.

35. In the end, Madero's attitude toward Castillo and Terrazas was the same that he assumed toward all revolutionaries after the end of the revolution. He asked the Zapatistas in the south and the Orozquistas in the north to turn over their weapons and return to their homeland, while he left the Porfirian generals and officers in their positions. The best Madero was able to offer Castillo was a job as watchman in Chapultepec Park; and Terrazas, the aforementioned offer as chief of police.

36. The revolutionaries of Chihuahua considered themselves defrauded by Francisco I. Madero and looked for other channels. Before Castillo decided to break with Maderismo, his closest associates had already done so.

37. On March 3, 1912, the troops that served the garrison in Chihuahua City withdrew recognition from the [federal] government. General Pascual Orozco assumed leadership over the revolutionary movement. Governor Abraham González went into hiding, and the legislature supported the revolutionary movement and named Felipe B. Gutiérrez interim governor. Thus a short Orozquista period began in Chihuahua that lasted a little more than three months. Before Orozco joined the anti-Madero movement, a rebellion in favor of Emilio Vázquez Gómez had begun in Cd. Juárez, with the participation of most of the principal chiefs associated with Orozco during the revolution of 1910.

On February 27, 1912, the Vazquistas had taken Cd. Juárez, which forced many Chihuahuenses to define their position with respect to Madero—among others, Pascual Orozco himself. On March 25, the revolutionaries issued the Plan de La Empacadora, signed first by Orozco. This document contained a recitation of all the errors of the Maderistas. In thirty-seven articles, the plan offered a blueprint for true change in the nation. With regard to the land issue, the plan stipulated the expropriation of all land that lay fallow, the redistribution of all nationalized and fallow lands, and the restitution of land stolen from its rightful owners.

In some of its provisions, the plan is more advanced than those of San Luis, Tacubaya, and Ayala. It is the plan of the Chihuahuenses against the government of Francisco I Madero, and it establishes an important precedent for the Constitution of 1917. According to Silva Herzog (*Breve historia*, 1:219–20), the constitution represents the philosophical culmination of seven years of civil struggle.

Juan Gualberto Amaya (op. cit., 380) believes that the anti-United States sentiment of the Plan de la Empacadora earned the Orozquista movement the opposition of the government of the United States, a determining factor in its defeat.

38. On March 24, government and Orozquista forces clashed at the Chihuahua-Coahuila border in a site known as Rellano. It was a very important battle because it amounted to an opportunity, speaking in military terms, for the rebels to reach the capital of the republic. Nonetheless, the Orozquista army could not advance far because of a lack

of weaponry and ammunition. As of March 14, the government of the United States had decreed a total embargo [against the Orozquistas].

39. The fortifications of Parral were very much embattled during those days. On March 20, Francisco Villa defeated the Orozquistas under the leadership of José de la Luz Soto. There was another battle on the 24th of the same month, and according to the official dispatches of that year, Villa once again defeated the Orozquistas, this time commanded by Emilio Campa.

40. For the description of this incident, see the text and notes on pp. 107–8.

41. The entire contingent stationed near Pedriceña was cut off from the main army and exposed to all kinds of problems after the two chiefs had died. Marcelo Caraveo (op. cit., 70) discusses this issue in the following manner:

> With the purpose of distracting the enemy, Pascual [Orozco] commissioned José Inés Salazar to cross the Sierra Mojada in a march toward Parras. At the same time, he ordered another column commanded by Colonels Abelardo Amaya and César Canales to take Pedriceña, Durango, which would cut the communication between Torreón and the city of Durango. In contrast to what happened to Salazar, who had no other choice than to return to his base, Amaya and Canales obtained victories at Velardeña and Pedriceña, although both perished in the latter combat.

42. The deaths of Amaya and Canales signified the irretrievable loss of two very important Orozquista chiefs. Both distinguished themselves by their firm revolutionary convictions and military ability. Without a doubt, this loss contributed significantly to the defeats that the Orozquistas would suffer during the following days—setbacks that proved decisive for the defeat of the movement.

43. After the triumph at Rellano on March 24, the Orozquista rebels were in good position to advance southward, and even to take the capital of the republic; however, it was not possible to do so due to the lack of weapons and ammunition. During the following days, President Madero named General Victoriano Huerta the new chief or the army, and Huerta traveled to Torreón on April 11 and immediately summoned all of the forces, forming the División del Norte [Division of the North]. On May 6, the División advanced toward the north. On May 9, the troops of General Rábago defeated the Orozquistas in Tlahualilo. Five days later, the Orozquista forces defeated the Federales in Pedriceña. On May 11 and 12, the battle in the station of Conejos resulted in the defeat of the rebel army, leaving hundreds of casualties on the battlefield. On May 22 and 23, the Orozquista movement was decisively defeated in the station of Rellano.

44. Juan Gualberto Amaya (op. cit., 375) makes the following commentary:

> The Chihuahuense rebel movement committed grave errors—not only political errors, but also within its own military organization, which lacked a harmonious base that would have given it the necessary consistency. Generally, all the armed groups in the various villages of the state were in agreement as to Madero's betrayal of his own Plan of San Luis Potosí, and all of them were motivated by the same

aim, to wit, the overthrow of someone whom they considered a false apostle. That was the most important point, but it was not sufficient because popular revolutions require a conscientious preparation that establishes the procedures to follow and clarifies the causes [for fighting], delineating the aims and principles so that they may be anchored in the conscience of the people. Orozco and his principal subordinate chiefs—all of them very young—were inexperienced; they did not understand how to approach political crossroads, and they found confidence and inspiration in their daring youth. Despite their vigorous power, the lack of experience made them vulnerable to committing serious errors, with fatal consequences.

45. In these notes, Castillo presents a depressing image of the Orozquistas, and he portrays some of the movement's principal chiefs as opportunistic and selfish. One must ask to what extent his opinion was colored by the frustration that Castillo felt in 1914, when he wrote his memoirs. What does become clear is that Orozquismo did not succeed in centralizing command and a coordination of the maneuvers. Various authors agree with Michael Meyer (op. cit., 95 and 104) regarding the fact that a scarcity of ammunition and armaments decisively damaged Orozco's army.

Meyer describes the defeat of Orozquismo in Bachimba in the following terms:

> At the end of June, General Orozco decided to fight in Bachimba. When the enemy forces began to prepare themselves for the encounter, the Orozquistas worried about the same problem that had made possible their defeat in the second battle of Rellano: the lack of arms and ammunition . . . [It was] a spent rebel force with few weapons that confronted the Federales on July 3, 1912. In surprising fashion, Orozco was able to do battle the entire day before finding himself compelled to order the retreat.

46. We have not found evidence that supports General Castillo's assertion regarding Orozco's supposed betrayal of the rebel movement. The definitive defeat of Orozquismo occurred on August 16, 1912, when the Federal forces captured Cd. Juárez, the place where the movement had begun the previous February. It is important to mention that in the course of the year 1912, and even more so, during the year 1913, Orozquismo and the public image of Pascual Orozco were the targets of a campaign of defamation and lies. The press of the United States and several journalists and writers from Mexico City contributed to this campaign.

47. Michael Meyer (op. cit., 109) relates that Pascual Orozco was wounded on September 11 during the Battle of Ojinaga, and that he traveled to the United States as a consequence, returning to Chihuahua during the first days of December. The same author believes that Orozquismo remained a significant threat to the government because of the decentralization of command, and he suggests that the movement could not have sustained itself after the defeat at Cd. Juárez if it had coordinated command under single leadership. Throughout January 1913, the Maderista General Antonio Rábago informed [the government] that the rebels were intensifying their guerrilla activities, and in mid-January, the Orozquistas once again threatened to attack Cd. Juárez and Chihuahua City.

48. At that time, Orozquismo had completely lost the initiative. Rojas, who had gathered more information and remained convinced that it no longer made sense to expose oneself to harm, only dedicated himself to avoid battles and risk that, according to his logic, would not yield any benefits to a cause in free fall.

49. According to Marcelo Caraveo (op. cit., 72),

> At that point, we began to feel the effects of the Orozquista manifesto against the North Americans, because it became more difficult with each passing day to obtain ammunition and medication. Faced with these circumstances, Pascual ordered the Orozquista troops to split into two columns: one would move toward Sonora under the command of Rojas, Campos, Argumedo, and Campa, and the other under the command of Orozco and myself. We moved toward the north, and shortly before arriving at the small town of Ahumada, we abandoned the trains and proceeded toward Ojinaga, a municipality that we conquered after dislodging Colonel Cruz Sánchez. Pascual [Orozco] set himself up in Ojinaga, and I marched toward the state of Coahuila with seven or eight hundred men.

In that state, the Federal army was already aware of Caraveo's presence. For several weeks, after crossing the desert, he did all that he could to sustain his battered army, returning to Chihuahuense territory with approximately 250 men. In his work, Caraveo recounts that during his crossing of the desert on the way back to Chihuahua, Luis Elizondo, the former personal secretary of don Abraham González, put a bullet in his head, having been tormented by thirst for several days. He also cites the case of Captain Muñoz, who slit open his veins for the same reason. That was the army that Máximo Castillo encountered in late 1912, to which he joined his small force.

50. On January 14, 1913, the *Mexican Herald*, trying to demonstrate Orozco's "depravity," published an article on the front page about the fate of the Federal general J. de Luz Blanco, whom the Orozquistas had "hung from a tree and riddled with bullets." Ten days later, the same newspaper published a retraction in small print, which pointed out that Blanco had been captured by the Orozquistas but freed unharmed (Meyer, op. cit., 106).

51. In his account of the revolution, Marcelo Caraveo (op. cit., 74) makes reference to a meeting with General Antonio Rábago, the military chief of Chihuahua, in early January 1913:

> . . . I received a communiqué from General Antonio Rábago . . . in which he asked to speak to me. I accepted the request and, accompanied by my subordinates, I met this military leader in Rancho Blanco in the northwest of Chihuahua. In the name of Madero, I was asked to surrender, because it was already useless and harmful for the country to continue this civil war. He offered that, should I accept his request, my rank of general would be recognized, and I would be able to continue in command of my troops . . . The offer was tempting, but I had to reject it, because as long as there were Orozquistas who remained standing, the fight needed to continue. After this interview, my troops offered to name me chief of the movement, but due to the uncertainty over whether Pascual [Orozco] remained alive, I refused the proposition.

52. The brothers Emilio and Francisco Vázquez Gómez belonged to the group of marginalized revolutionaries: first, through Maderismo, and then, by confronting both Huerta and Carranza. Throughout the period 1911–19, the brothers Vázquez Gómez represented the leadership alternative for the rebel groups in the north and south. As late as 1919, a few days before his death, General Emiliano Zapata made a proposal to President Venustiano Carranza in the name of the revolutionary movement of the south. According to the proposal, Carranza would resign and accept a government of national harmony directed by someone who enjoyed national prestige on account of his honor as well as his progressive and egalitarian ideas. The leader whom Zapata proposed was Dr. Francisco Vázquez Gómez. (See, in the appendix to the Spanish-language edition of this work, the text of the letter from General Emiliano Zapata to the editor of the newspaper, *La Patria*, April 28, 1919, under the title of "Una carta del general Zapata").

53. Marcelo Caraveo (op. cit., 76) relates this event as follows:

Days after the events in the Ciudadela, Pascual and I were called to Mexico City. It was in February 1913, more or less. Pascual was in the company of his personal secretary, José Córdoba, as well as Luis Esther Estrada, Alfonso Castañeda, Crisóforo and Miguel Caballero, Miguel and Tomás Chacon, Juan Prieto, and others whom I do not remember right this minute. Although I was afraid that [the government] was playing a dirty trick, I accompanied the group with all of my troops . . . Once there, Pascual, Argumedo, Campos, and I were brought before Huerta. With large, dark glasses and a husky voice, he began to tell us that even though we had once needed to continue fighting to fulfill our duty, there was no reason to remain distanced [from the government] during the present circumstances. It was time, he said, to make peace for the benefit of the nation. The interview lasted one hour, and Huerta was pleasant and courteous throughout. Nothing definitive came out of the meeting, but I think it served as a way for Huerta to get to know us, and for us to get to know Huerta.

. . . After a few days of not seeing Pascual, who was in constant discussions and banquets with Huerta, I left him a message with his personal secretary telling him that we were retiring to Chihuahua in view of his indifference toward those who had followed and helped him the most. The message told him to let us know if he needed us. At that time, Huerta had already offered Pascual the supreme command of the border states of Sonora, Chihuahua, and Coahuila, a task he never completed.

54. The vacillations of *licenciado* Emilio Vázquez Gómez and Máximo Castillo must be considered in the context of the general situation that Huerta's military coup produced in Mexico. At the beginning of 1913, Madero's government found itself weakened by all of the divisions that it had suffered. In addition to the fact that the government did not control the opposition in the north or the south, the political spheres of the capital were rife with conspiracies. A number of alliances formed that awaited the demise of Madero's government. Even the leaders most involved in the birth of the Constitutionalist movement vacillated, in the beginning, about whether to recognize the Huerta government. Such was the case with Venustiano Carranza, who has been accused of conspiring against

Madero; some even claim that Carranza initially recognized Victoriano Huerta's usurper government. See Manuel Bonilla, *Diez años de Guerra*, and Alfonso Junco, *Carranza y los orígenes de su rebelión*.

55. At that moment, Máximo Castillo defined his position with full clarity. Against the decision of all the Orozquista chiefs, Emilio Vázquez Gómez did not recognize Huerta. The relationship between Vázquez Gómez and Zapata definitely draws in Castillo, and from that moment on, he took up the project and agrarista ideals championed by the Zapatista revolutionaries.

56. See the text of the commission in the appendix to the Spanish-language edition of this work.

57. The search for this document has been fruitless. One presumes that it posits the struggle for land as a principal aspect of the revolution, and that it prioritizes the immediate redistribution of the large haciendas. In addition, this part of Castillo's account raises several questions. Why were Salazar and Rojas interested in involving Castillo in the movement supporting Huerta? Because of their friendship or comradeship? Because of a sense of doubt or culpability? Because of the leadership position that Castillo had acquired among the revolutionary forces?

58. Castillo represented the most important force in the state that did not recognize Huerta. Villa's forces were very much inferior. Nonetheless, Villa did not agree to join up with Castillo. What were his reasons for rejecting Castillo? We can mention a few possible causes. First, Villa may not have been certain that Castillo had definitely broken away from Orozquismo. Second, as we have mentioned above, Villa did not accept Castillo's agrarista principles, especially concerning the immediate redistribution of the haciendas and great estates without major paperwork. [As Villa knew, this program would] antagonize the government of the United States. In addition, Villa always believed that the redistribution of land should be postponed until after the victory of his army: to the contrary, who would fight the revolution if people were busy sowing their crops? Finally, Villa surely thought that the principal beneficiaries [of land reform] should be the men who had taken up arms, to wit, the soldiers of the División del Norte, the Zapatistas, and the other allies of Villismo. Castillo's objectives ran counter to all of these. Given that his attempts at unification coincided with his redistribution of land, the second hypothesis appears the most likely.

59. See the "Deed of the Distribution of the Hacienda of San Luis" in the appendix to the Spanish-language edition of this work. The hacienda of San Luis was located in the municipality of San Buenaventura. In the Registro Público de la Propiedad, it appeared with 328,989 hectares; it was also known as "the nose."

60. General Federico Cervantes, the author of a well-documented book about Villismo, mentions that a Villista contingent defeated the *colorados* of José Parra in Casas Grandes on June 29, 1913. See Cervantes, *Francisco Villa y la revolución* (Mexico City: Alonso, 1960), 54. In fact, this military engagement marked the beginning of the decline of Castillo's army. Within the logic of the Chihuahuense anti-Huertistas, it did not make sense for Villa and Castillo to fight each other. In the eyes of the people, the Villista campaign inspired more confidence. Little by little, Villismo attracted more troops, while Castillo's contingent began to diminish with every blow it received.

61. The redistributed haciendas were abandoned because the campesinos understood that a distribution without military backing, and without force, did not imply any guarantee. Little by little, the initiative of Castillo, who had redistributed land two months earlier than Lucio Blanco in Tamaulipas, found itself diluted.

62. Braulio Hernández and Castillo had walked the same revolutionary ground since 1910. What he writes in these lines regarding the revolutionary deviations of [Braulio Hernández] is surprising. Although we tried hard to find evidence regarding the whereabouts of Hernández after 1913, we did not find any information. But one day, looking at microfilm of the newspaper *La Patria*, we found in the interior pages a full-page advertisement of the North American company Tampico Petroleum Pipeline and Refining in which the company introduces its leadership. Its secretary and treasurer was Professor Braulio Hernández, about whom the advertisement said the following:

> A well-known Mexican of good reputation . . . he was a professor in institutions of higher learning in the Mexican republic and in the state of Texas in the United States . . . Mr. Hernández lived in El Paso, Texas, for more than seven years, and captivated the sympathies of numerous friends, among them professionals and persons of irreproachable reputation. Most recently, the gentleman was a professor of one of the foremost educational institutions of the city of Dallas, Texas.

63. Among the documents consulted in the library of the University of Texas–El Paso, we found a very interesting notice published by the *El Paso Morning Times* on February 20, 1913. According to this source, the Villistas had reported Castillo and his comrades [to the North American authorities], and a Villista detachment had participated along with North American forces to [apprehend Castillo and his men]. The El Paso press gave detailed information about Castillo's detention (see information in the appendix to the Spanish-language edition of this work).

64. See Castillo's declarations to a reporter of the newspaper *El Paso Morning Times*, published on February 20, 1914, especially those appearing under the heading "Castillo's Confessions."

65. When the El Paso press published the notice of Máximo Castillo's arrest, it also announced that he would be imprisoned along with General J. Inés Salazar, an inmate of Fort Bliss since January 10, 1914. After Francisco Villa's army defeated the Huertista-Orozquista troops in Ojinaga, Salazar crossed the river with three thousand soldiers. He was detained by the North American army and isolated in a special prison cell, in which Castillo would later join him.

66. This dialogue shows us a very cynical Salazar. It is necessary to point out that his was not an isolated case. Rojas, Porras, Caraveo, Alanís, Campa, Orpinel, Del Toro, and many other Orozquista chiefs who had joined the revolution under the impulse of the Magonista program later shifted to new currents of thought. But almost all those who allied with Huertismo found themselves outside the revolutionary current, isolated and confused.

67. In this regard, a few newspapers from El Paso, Texas, published notices about the mistreatment of the Mexicans confined to Fort Bliss as reflected in a document from

the Mexican consul in El Paso, sent on March 27, 1914, to General Francisco Castro. The document makes reference to the notice published that same day in *México Libre*, an independent newspaper. The notice announced the following:

Prisoner Tortured in Fort Bliss. Yesterday, a "prick" hit a poor soldier among the prisoners in Fort Bliss with the flat side of a sword. After hitting him, he tied [the prisoner] to a post using a wire. This is a very humanitarian proceeding according to the way that the North Americans understand humanitarianism with respect to our nationals.

I transcribe this for your attention with the request to let me know whether this notice is true. I renew to you the assurances of my highest consideration. (Photocopy of the document in the personal archive of Jesús Vargas Valdés.)

68. According to a notice in the newspaper *Vida Nueva* from May 6, 1914, Jesús San Martín was also accused of having participated in the explosion of the train in Cumbre.

69. The original manuscript of the memoir ends here.

THE DÉNOUEMENT

1. The family did not record the exact date of Máximo Castillo's passing in Havana, Cuba. We believe that the death occurred between February and April 1919. A document from the Administración General de Bienes Intervenidos with the date of February 17, 1919, contains the order to release from confiscation his house in the Santo Niño neighborhood. The name of his wife appears as María de Jesús Flores de Castillo. Later, in other documents from May 1919 relating to the same matter, it appears as María de Jesús Flores viuda de Castillo.

INDEX

CPSIA information can be obtained
at www.ICGtesting.com
Printed in the USA
LVHW032248081121
702781LV00007B/1438